Journey of the Groovy Goddess
Finding My Authentic Self

Lacey Dawn Jackson

Copyright © 2015 LaceyHealing

All rights reserved.

ISBN-13: 978-0989641807 (LaceyHealing)
ISBN-10: 0989641805

All rights reserved. No part of this book may be reproduced in any form, except for the inclusion of brief quotations in review, without permission in writing from the author and by acknowledging the author when doing so.

Cover: author's private collection of pictures taken while in Ireland: An Searrach, Kinard, Lispole
Picture below: Mother Mary Statue at a Holy Well

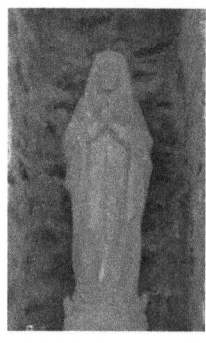

LaceyHealing

I dedicate this book to all my clients with whom I have shared aspects of my life in order to inspire them in following their intuitive heart.

CONTENTS

Dedication	3
Contents	4
Acknowledgments	5
Preface	6
Prologue	9
So It Begins	11
Being an Adult	54
Life Begins Again	76
White Picket Fence	86
Running Away from Me	102
Awakening to My Own Needs	151
Wolf's in Sheep's Clothing	196
Waking up to My True Self	212
I Can See Clearly Now	253
After Thoughts	280
About Author	289

ACKNOWLEDGMENTS

Thanks to mom, dad and sister for accepting me as I am. A big thanks and lots of love to my two sons who I love more than I can even express!

Thank you to all my 12Family members for their love, blessings and support. Thank you to CA Brooks for being a great editor.

I have been blessed by many friendships that are very important to me. Without you (and you know who you are) I would not be the person I am today. Thank you!

Thank You Red for the support and the lovely surroundings you graciously shared with me while I finished this book.

PREFACE

When I look at myself today, I see a Groovy Goddess in tune with my life purpose and devoted to helping others find theirs. I'm surrounded by healthy and supportive relationships, have a job I love, and enjoy life to the fullest by expressing who I am every day. But it wasn't always like this. In fact, it was <u>nothing</u> like this. Read on to see a glimpse of what my life used to be like and what it took to make me who I am today. If you are unhappy with who and where you are, you can change too, regardless of your circumstances. I know, because I've done it!

Because I didn't know how to handle all of the psychic information (and we are all psychic) that had been coming to me my whole life, I became numb and shut out any intuitive information I received. I was used to feeling bad about myself because I believed I couldn't decipher the guidance that was screaming at me to make changes.

I began to work on myself taking one step forward and sometimes two steps back. I was determined to keep going. I felt from within there was something out there for me. I didn't even know where 'out there' was, but I had to find it. So I went searching and many of my choices didn't make the path easy. I was feeling uncomfortable within myself, which in itself was enough to lead me down many and various paths. But doesn't it take us all a few knocks on the head to learn our most valuable lessons in this Earth School?

This story involves the dysfunction, the magic, and the healing I went through in finding my authentic self. Through my trials, I have come to understand, love, and nurture myself through gentleness, understanding, and realizing we are not all perfect.

The first step to healing and finding our own voice is sometimes a long and weary road but it makes us much stronger. I believe I have gone through these experiences so I can be a better advocate for people going through difficulties, since I understand the dynamics first hand. If only one person reads this and feels inspired, or it gives them the gumption to get out of bed and live another day, it has been worth it to me.

For a very long time I lived in fear of telling my story. Throughout the years many people, who knew only parts of my story, told me I needed to share it because my story inspired them. I would always smile as a little voice inside my head (probably my ego) would say "if you only knew the whole story". At the same time a voice (my higher groovy self) kept telling me I could no longer deny it; it was time to tell my story.

As I sat down to write, memories of my life raced within my mind. How was I to begin with such a seemingly huge task? How is it possible to plow through all the information flooding my mind? How can I face and move through the horror I feel about subjecting myself and my loved ones to parts of this story?

I realize telling my story may open up a new barrage of judgments toward me for the decisions and the choices I made as I navigated through life searching for my authentic self. Since I have already judged all of my actions at one time or another, there are absolutely no more judgments to be made. So with a little kicking and screaming, and a lot of love and kindness towards myself, I tell my story. Keep an open mind and heart, as this story I hold dear to my heart, I pass to your heart this day.

Blessings to YOU!!

Lacey Dawn Jackson

PROLOGUE

It was a warm summer day, late afternoon in the midst of the 4th of July holiday weekend. My two boys were outside playing with the other kids in the apartment complex. A parade of kids running in and out of my small apartment left the door open. I didn't mind. The fresh breeze was warm and the intoxicating aroma of salt air cleared my head. I was putting clothes away in the bedroom when the boys ran in yelling, "There are men at our door and one is a policeman!"

Just then I heard a knock. I walked out of the bedroom. As I turned the corner, I saw two men standing at the door. Behind them was a policeman. My heart started pounding. They identified themselves as FBI and told me they were here to ask me questions about Sam Russen and the disappearance of a 9-year old girl who had been missing for over 48 hours. They asked me if they could search my apartment before questioning me. I invited them in and they spread out looking through the two bedrooms, the big walk-in closet, bathroom and the kitchen. My two boys and a couple of the neighborhood girls were standing around looking from one FBI agent to another and back at the policeman. I asked the kids to go back outside to play and shut the door behind them as they ran out full of excitement and chatter.

The police officer excused himself and went outside. I motioned to the FBI agents to have a seat as I sat back in a chair. I scooted to the edge of the chair, somehow too uncomfortable to be at ease in this situation. They wanted to know the whereabouts of my ex boyfriend, Sam, otherwise known as Sam Russen. I felt my heart skip a beat and sink into my stomach. I told them it had been over a week since I had any communication with him and that it had been over the phone. It had not been a pleasant conversation. Sam wanted to see my son and I was making it difficult for him. It had been over a month since we had seen him. Sam said he missed me and wished I would come around more often, if only to visit his mom. His mother was hoping we'd figure this relationship thing out, since she believed I was the best thing that had ever happened to him; and she told him so.

I didn't want to be any part of his life. Six chaotic years was more than enough for me. I was focusing on my boys, my job, and delving into a new life without the turmoil I left ten months earlier. I must have taken a little too long to answer, because one of the FBI agents asked me again if I had any idea where he might be. Since it was the holiday weekend, I figured he was more than likely down at Rainbow Valley. Rainbow Valley was known as a place where old "Dead Heads", modern-day hippies, and wanderers hung out. The 4th of July weekend was sure to include a big party with many musical bands playing on stage, as well as lots of vendors peddling their arts and crafts. It would be in full swing this weekend. Because Sam was a musician, it was highly likely he was there. The FBI agent asked me if they could call on me again if they had further questions. Nodding my head, I said "yes". I was more than willing to help out if I could. I silently prayed for the little girl as I watched the men walk down the sidewalk.

My life with Sam was never easy. I had finally mustered up the courage to break free in an attempt to forge a better life for myself and my two sons. The shadow of the past was once again reaching out to remind me of everything I had gone through with Sam and of other experiences in relationships that had brought me to this point in my life. As I looked over the beautiful Puget Sound, I swore I wouldn't let this latest episode draw me back into that chaos.

SO IT BEGINS

My mom was 19 years old, my dad 23 when I came into the world one August morning well before the early bird was ready to get the first worm of the day. I was only 6 hours old when my dad and a nursing student friend, who went to school with my mom, drove me up to the Children's Hospital in Seattle. I was born with a cleft pallet and needed surgery to close the roof of my mouth which opened directly into my nasal passage. I was in the hospital for about a month before I was able to come home for the first time. I healed quickly and was a good natured little baby.

At nine months old I went back east with my parents in my dad's Lincoln Continental. My parents had less than a hundred dollars and a gas credit card in their pocket. That was enough to get us where we were going. We were headed to Vermont to meet my grandma and grandpa along with other relatives. We stayed for a couple of weeks then drove back home to Washington State.

A couple of years later we drove back to Vermont, this time in our Volkswagen bus. My sister was just a baby; and I was three years old. We ended up bringing my grandpa back to Washington with us. My grandma and grandpa hadn't been together for many years and my grandpa had nothing keeping him there.

Grandpa was a farmer by trade and could easily find work on a farm close to us in Washington. My grandpa's nickname was Stub because he had been in a car accident when he was younger and lost his right arm, leaving just a stub long enough to make us kids giggle when he used it to wave to us. Our landlord at the time had a farm out in the country not too far from where we lived. My grandpa was given a place to live on the farm and started working for him. My parents dreamed of buying a piece of property and building a little house for my grandpa. We were going to get cows, chickens, ducks and pigs so my grandpa would have something to keep him busy. My mom planned on having a garden so we could eat fresh vegetables.

My dad had been out of the military for just over three years while my mom was working at the hospital as a nurse. They lived from paycheck to paycheck, my dad getting work wherever he could. He worked as a car salesman and he delivered papers. He worked as a janitor. He worked at a paper mill. Many times he had a couple jobs at the same time. He had his sights set on a factory that made aluminum cans because the benefits were good and the pay was very fair. He checked in at the factory every week to see if they were hiring. Meanwhile my mom made an impression on one of the surgeons at the hospital and was asked if she wanted to work in his office as his nurse. She immediately said yes. My dad had become a familiar face at the factory and was also offered a job. They were getting closer to their goal of buying land.

My mom's cousin, Mary Ann, lived near the water in Olympia. Occasionally, I spent the night with her and her boyfriend. I loved going over there because we would walk along the shore of the Puget Sound – a body of salt water leading out to the ocean. When the tide was out, we would search the shore looking at shells and other sea life that lay upon the sand and rocks. Mary Ann was the first person who introduced me to dance. She would turn on music and we would dance away. It always left me feeling so full and happy whenever I could spend time walking along the water and dancing to my heart's content.

These memories fill my heart with joy. Memories such as mine, of dancing and walking along the shore are the ones that nourish us throughout our lives. These are the first memories of fulfillment and happiness. It is very important we hold on to these memories. They help us when we are struggling to find our way through life's challenges. Think back into your childhood. What activities do you remember playing or doing? Make a list of them. Also write down the memory that goes with the activity.

When I was in the first grade, my parents' dream of purchasing a piece of property out in the country finally came true. The land they chose was close enough to the freeway to enable my parents to get to work in a reasonable amount of time. My dad spent time getting the land ready to build a little house for my grandpa.

Eventually we planned to move into our own place on the property. My sister and I would go down to the property with my dad while he would work on the land. I enjoyed riding my bike up and down the driveway and along the old country road. I loved how fresh the air smelled and how the soft breeze blew through my hair as I pedaled my bike. I felt the thrill of excitement as I gathered speed riding my bike down the hill in front of our property. I felt like I was flying and as free as a bird.

I was seven years old, when early one morning, I climbed on my bike and rode off down the hill. My front wheel must have hit a rock. All of a sudden, my bike started swaying from side to side as I continued to gather speed. Soon after, everything went blank. The next thing I remember was waking up in my dad's arms. We were on the highway and my dad's friend was driving. We were approaching town and I was feeling very dazed and uncomfortable. I felt dizzy and could see I was covered in blood. This made me want to throw up.

We took the next exit and drove around the lake to where my mom was working at a medical clinic. My dad carried me inside. As soon as I saw my mom I started crying even more. I was scared.

The staff at the clinic took one look at me and immediately rushed me into an exam room. I needed to have my lip sewn back together. They prepped me by cleaning the injury and picking rocks out of my lip and face. They asked my mom to leave the room and I could hear her screaming in the back ground. She didn't want to leave me. A nurse calmly told her she would be right there with me. It would be all right. I had lost one of my front teeth so while they worked sewing my lip back together and repairing my nose, my dad drove back to the property to find my tooth. Lucky for me he found my tooth with the root still intact. The doctors put my tooth back into my gum and placed a plaster-like material on the top row of my teeth to hold the tooth in place in hopes the root would take hold.

When I got home, I looked into the mirror and screamed. I didn't recognize myself. I got upset every time I passed a mirror. There was a steel splint over my nose taped to my forehead and across each cheek. My swollen upper lip reached far beyond my nose and had lots of black stitches poking out of it. My eyes were black from the trauma to my nose. I had to drink with a straw and couldn't have any solid foods because of an awful tasting bridge that was fastened to my upper teeth to hold the tooth in place. My parents ended up covering all the mirrors in the house so I wouldn't look at myself. I felt terrible. I could only ingest liquid or food my mom had prepared in a blender. I was fortunate I didn't have to go too long without eating solid foods. But I remember how miserable I felt. I had a constant headache and my face hurt. I was frustrated that I couldn't look at myself in the mirror. I would sneak a peek whenever I could which would bring me back to tears. The vision of how ugly I appeared would stay etched in my memory as I fell asleep. As much as my parents reassured me I would be fine and would look beautiful, I found it odd in light of the evidence I saw in the mirror. I knew I didn't look beautiful. Being a child, the present moment was the only time I could imagine. I was well on my way to feeling less than adequate and establishing a dislike for the way I looked. My self esteem was already taking a beating.

Traumatic events often plant a belief within us that we are not even aware of until many years later. It can sometimes be revealed through counseling or by reflecting on the meaning of our behavior and actions. The memory of seeing and disliking my swollen face in the mirror stayed with me for many years. I avoided looking at myself; and when I did look, I was often filled with feelings of disdain and negativity. Do you remember what you felt like as a child? What is your earliest memory of your own self esteem? What were some of your own thoughts about yourself?

After my grandpa's house was finished, he moved in and soon my parents found a single wide trailer for sale and moved it onto the property. I was very excited to have my own bedroom. There would be animals and a garden with lots of vegetables.

I ran in the fields. I climbed the trees. I fished for crawdads. I looked for periwinkles in the creek that ran through the back of our property. I inhaled the scent of the trees as the wind gently blew. I couldn't wait to get outside on sunny days to run and hide in the fields. At night I would tuck myself further down in my bed when I heard the coyotes howling from across the valley. Once in awhile a pack would be howling from just a field away. They would take turns crying out an eerie and haunting song. I would grab my dog Larry, a scruffy white poodle and burrow even deeper into the covers to feel safe. I always loved hearing the howls even though I knew they were on the hunt for food which sometimes would be a cat or a rabbit. I always prayed it wouldn't be any of our cats.

My parents purchased animals for my grandfather to care for. We started with a couple of calves. The menagerie grew with the addition of chickens, ducks, and rabbits. My favorite animals to arrive on our little farm were the pigs. Our first was named Marsha and we would ride around the cage on her back. As she would root and stomp in the mud, I joined her in the pen wearing my rubber boots. I loved climbing into her pig pen with her and sitting there while she oinked and grunted at me. Her first litter of piglets included Wilbur. We named Wilber after the famous pig in the popular book, Charlotte's Web.

Wilbur was the runt of the litter and was injured when Marsha accidentally stepped on him. My mom brought him into the house and stitched him up. While he recovered, we kept Wilbur in the house with us. My sister and I were tickled about that. We took turns feeding him his bottle. He suckled and grunted as the milk ran down his chin. As Wilbur grew, he scratched at the door just like the dogs to let us know he wanted to come in or go outdoors. Wilber had become part of the family. When I was eight years old I insisted on getting a horse so I could ride him in the fields. Unfortunately, when I discovered go-carts and mini-bikes a few years later, the horse didn't get ridden any longer.

I remember sometimes when I was playing, I would get this feeling of being here before. I felt like I was just 'coming to' as if I had been asleep and just woke up to my surroundings. Everything appeared brighter and fresher. It was as if I had just arrived on the scene and was looking around for the very first time. This confused me. I wondered if anyone else felt this way; but I had no idea how to explain it. I ended up keeping it to myself. Sometimes I worried about it and hoped there was nothing wrong with me. These feelings happened when I least expected it and for no apparent reason. Now I understand these feelings and experiences. It was a feeling of wholeness. It was a feeling of peace. It was a feeling of being aware of something bigger than myself. It was also a feeling of being totally in the present. It's the feeling of God.

When we are in a meditative state such as being outdoors, running in the fields, and thinking nothing of the past and nothing in the future, but only what is going on in that moment, we will bring on that feeling of oneness with everything. It is experience of wholeness, knowing we are all connected to something bigger than ourselves. As we get older, this feeling unfortunately often fades and is replaced with worries about the future and the stresses of everyday life. What do you do to bring yourself into the present moment? Getting outdoors, sitting quietly and being aware of what is around us here and now can bring us into a peaceful way which can invoke the feeling of God and fulfillment.

Other impactful memories from my childhood involve experiences with eating, food, and body image. I witnessed my mom, my babysitters and every woman around me doing some new diet that promised to give them the body of their dreams. The models in television commercials were always very skinny women. The beauty products advertised were guaranteed to make us prettier. If we were to attract a man, we would need this beauty product or that diet plan. The message may have been subliminal but it was clear; we were not good enough. It was no wonder I learned to think I was less than adequate and I needed to improve my body in order to be accepted.

Food was my first addiction. I grew up on processed foods because it was all the rage and heavily advertised on television. TV dinners and Hostess cakes were a must in every household. Boxed macaroni and cheese was a staple. Nothing stopped me from wanting everything yummy advertised on television. One of my favorite things to do was go grocery shopping. I always begged my mom for the sugary treats. My body couldn't get enough of them.

We were a meat and potatoes kind of family; and we also ate the vegetables we grew in our garden. (Squash was my favorite!) Main meals always had some kind of meat, usually out of our freezer, from the animals we raised. It seems odd now, as I look back at the calves and pigs we raised. We played with them and we ended up having them on our dinner table. One time as we were eating dinner which consisted of roast pork, mashed potatoes and gravy, my sister asked quite nonchalantly, "Is this Marsha we are eating? Neither my mom nor my dad said anything. I vaguely remember the nursery rhyme "Mary had a little lamb", but nowhere in the story do I remember that she ate it.

When I was in kindergarten, I remember opening my first can of tomato soup. I stood on a chair in front of the stove and with my mom's assistance stirred while it heated. My love for cooking had been established. As I got older, I couldn't wait for my parents to go to work. I would experiment with cooking things. Sugar was the main ingredient. I was already hooked on the feeling of the sugar going through my system and I knew I wanted more. I didn't understand why I was eating so much, nor did I think about it while I ate whatever I prepared. I was actually feeding my addiction to sugar and I would do anything to get it. I would sneak food and hide it in my room so I knew that I wouldn't go without. I ate more when there was stress in the house. I ate more when there were celebrations in the house. I ate more whenever I could. I was lucky I was also active and didn't expand as much as I could have. I spent most of my days outside running all over the hillside. Little did I know I was artificially feeding a void I felt within.

Food is all around us. We need food for energy and strength and to survive. Many times we do not know what foods are good for us, especially if we are influenced by the media. It looks so good on television; it must be good for us, right? I realize now much of my emptiness I tried to fill with food such as sugar that only aggravated my moods and had a negative impact on the way I felt. What are your memories of food or addiction? This might include your own issue or a problem belonging to someone around you. Thinking back, do you remember how it made you feel?

Despite my growing uneasiness and dysfunctional attitudes toward food and my body, I continued to experience a feeling of "oneness" I did not understand or know how to explain. I also sensed the presence of spirits and people no one else could see. I was haunted by the feeling of being an outsider, and the feeling of never really belonging or running with a pack. Eating, and later smoking, drinking alcohol, and doing drugs seemed to keep these feelings at bay, at least temporarily.

We are all born with intuitive gifts and a guardian angel. Although some of us remember early experiences with psychic abilities, intuition, and interacting with angels or guardian spirits, a much greater number of people forget these childhood experiences as they grow older. Some of us are scared by the reactions of others when we share these experiences and choose to just shut up. Often adults are not receptive; or are not able to adequately help us understand what is going on. Fortunately things are changing. There is a wider understanding and growing acceptance and more people are able to remember and hold onto their experiences with angels and intuition. What are some of your earliest memories of intuition or angelic sightings?

When I was in 3rd grade, I took accordion lessons. My teacher said I had a natural gift and could be excellent if I would practice more. Playing in a recital in front of many people at a church was my first experience of stage fright. I remember I was so excited and scared at the same time. When I started playing, I forgot about the fear. Afterwards, I really looked forward to staying after school on Thursdays to attend my lessons. The downside was the kids teased me for playing such a weird instrument. I tried to hide it; but inevitably someone would see me practicing and would tease me the next day. The teasing hurt a lot. All I wanted to do was fit in with the other kids. Eventually I abandoned practicing and my lessons all together. I just wanted to fit in. Think about the times you were persuaded to not do something you really wanted to do. How did it make you feel?

I learned to drive in my parents' little yellow Datsun when I was about eight years old. They would let me drive around the yard for hours to practice. When the neighbor girls came to play, I would go down to their house and pick them up and drive them back home in the Datsun. We would first circle around the yard a few times and then drive up and down the driveway before leaving to take them home. Sometimes I think I must have gone through a full tank of gas in a day just driving around with my sister and the neighbor kids. It was my earliest memory of feeling cool with my friends and being in control.

When I was about nine years old we took another trip to Vermont. We drove the economical Datsun, stayed in cheap hotels along the way, and ate McDonalds which we kids loved. In those days there was no such thing as the "dollar menu". Everything on the menu was under a dollar. It was a very inexpensive way to travel. We spent hours and days in the car. Sometimes I thought we would never get to where we were going. I couldn't look out my side window for very long at a time, because I would start to feel car sick. Soon even the thought of it, made me want to throw up even more. Needless to say, I was not a happy camper. Probably out of boredom I would start to bother my sister. We had this imaginary line in the middle of our seat and I would put my hand slightly over the line, thus making her mad because I was on her side of the car. Other times she would do the same. We would start fighting about who was hogging the back seat which resulted in frustrating my parents. It seemed to make time pass quicker though.

For days we drove in what seemed to be a straight line with the same scenery over and over as far as the eye could see. Occasionally there was a stand of trees or a plateau of land in the far distance. The terrain was dotted with an occasional house or very small town that looked deserted as we sped by. I was half asleep that morning as we got into the car. It was still dark when I left my comfortable bed at the motel, still early before anyone else was awake. My dad wanted to get a head start on the day because we had a long way to go through Montana heading to South Dakota, our next stop being Mt Rushmore. As we drove, the sun was coming up and the hue in the sky was beautifully bright pinks, oranges and yellows set against the land so flat. It was a color show that enthralled me through half closed eyes.

We were about half way through Montana when I heard my parents talking about stopping soon to get a bite to eat. I was ready to get out of the car to stretch my legs and to finally go to the bathroom. I had to go several miles back but was waiting for my sister to express the need to go before I did. We passed a sign and I wondered what it said. I asked and my mom said, "Crow Reservation". We started slowing down and pulled into a restaurant parking lot. As we got out, I noticed everyone looked like Indians I had seen in Westerns on television. Except these people weren't on horses, nor did they have feathers in their hair; although their hair was long and black and they were very dark skinned. I wondered if they were wild like they were depicted on television, hooting and hollering, out of control as they galloped their horses through town. I didn't see anything that resembled television.

We walked into the restaurant and an older lady approached the table with menus and coffee. She had kind dark eyes, with dark wrinkly skin. She wore a big braid of hair down the center of her back. She had turquoise stones hanging from her ears. I was very curious as I looked around and caught myself staring. Later when my family talked about this part of the trip, my mom would joke and say because I was wearing braids and was dark skinned, everyone probably thought I was a little Indian girl. I secretly hoped so. I certainly looked the part.

Later that night as the sun was starting to set, we arrived in the Black Hills of the Dakotas. I remember feeling strangely connected to the lands around us. It felt like I had been there before. There was also an eerie feeling in the air. We had arrived just days after the horrific Black Hills flood which caused extensive damage to the Rapid City area. Between the two feelings – familiarity with the land and fear caused by the flooding – I didn't sleep well that night. I tossed and turned and dreamed of water rushing towards me. In the dream I was also aware of a very kind but powerful presence I couldn't explain.

We woke up very early the next morning to go to Mount Rushmore. When we arrived, it was very foggy and the presidents' faces were obscured. There were flurries of tourists from all over the world gathered to view the monument. It was the first time I heard so many different languages spoken around me at one time. What I remember the most is another monument called Mount Crazy Horse that shined through the mist. Even though it wasn't finished, its magnificence struck a chord deep within me. It was as if I understood something and its significance was deeper and more meaningful than I could put into words. It left an indelible impression upon me. Whenever I think back on this part of my life, I have a palpable feeling I can actually feel in my body. Many years later I experienced this very tangible reaction when I discovered a personal connection to this monument and to a man who became a spiritual mentor to me.

In the evenings, the adults sat and visited while I played horse shoes with my aunt who was just a few years older than me. My aunt ended up coming back with us to spend the summer. I was excited until we started back on our long journey. The back seat of the Datsun had just gotten smaller. I alternated between feeling like I was going to explode or was slowly suffocating because of the lack of space in the back seat. By the time we arrived at Yellowstone National Park, I was green. I could hardly wait to get out of the car. My mistake that morning was eating the rest of the bag of Cheetos that had been left in the car from the day before. As we drove along a winding highway, I knew my dad had better stop the car soon before I threw up all over everyone. He did stop in the nick of time just as I poured myself out of the car and onto the side of the road and vomited all the Cheetos I had eaten.

Needless to say, for the rest of the day, I was feeling less than satisfactory. Feelings of nausea spoiled most of the day. I didn't enjoy seeing Old Faithful erupt or all the animals in the park. The only time I felt any kind of excitement was when we spotted a big moose right outside the gate as we were leaving. Much later I would discover that moose would prove to be one of my totem allies in tough times when I needed stamina.

One of the ways we can get closer to spirit is through the animals that come into our lives. I learned to call upon totem animals in meditation. During challenging times I asked totem animals to show up in my vision. When I got older, I used a deck of animal cards and would pick a card and read about the animal and try to apply its meaning and message to what was going on in my life at the time. Many times it provided the strength I was lacking. What animal are you drawn to? Look up the symbolic meaning of that animal and ask for its strength to help you.

I was relieved when we reached a motel that evening. I went right to bed. I was exhausted. Suitably traumatized, I didn't eat any more Cheetos for a long time afterwards. By this time, I think my parents were as anxious to get home as we were, because I don't remember stopping anywhere else to sight see for the rest of the trip. Every day proved to be a challenge in the back seat of that small yellow Datsun for another reason. Not only was it cramped with three girls riding in the back seat, but every so often someone in the car would pass gas filling the car with a rotten egg smell. I know for sure it wasn't me.

It was summer vacation when a couple of young men came calling and invited us to attend a week long bible school especially for young people. Since the church was located less than half of a mile from my house, I talked my parents into letting me attend. I could easily walk to the church so they wouldn't have to worry about taking or picking me up or altering their work schedules. My family didn't make it a practice of going to church so when this opportunity came up, I was intent on going. I kept a little bible near my bed and would read it at night. Even though I really didn't understand it, I still felt the need to study about God. I was excited, but also a little afraid since I heard God was to be feared. This would be the perfect time to get some of my questions answered about who God was. I was so excited about going to bible school for the week.

Vividly I remember sitting in a very little classroom in the small church. The room was cramped with the seven of us including the youth minister. When he spoke the words "we should fear God", I felt my body tighten. It didn't resonate with me and I was confused. As a matter of fact, I felt myself get angry. I had come to find out who this God character was, and without even knowing him, I was supposed to be afraid of him? I didn't expect to be told to fear him right off the bat.

As a youngster I was quick to goof off and bible school was no exception. When I interrupted the youth minister and made the comment "I'm not afraid of anyone, especially God", he made it known he didn't appreciate my disruption. I asked, "Why am I supposed to be afraid of God?" The young man got very short with me and told me to not disturb the class again. I left that day frustrated and very confused as to why I would need to fear God. The minister had not explained anything to me including why I should fear God. Not surprisingly, I decided not to go back the next day. I also decided I was not going to fear someone I didn't know. I decided I would just play out in the fields and in the forest instead. Little did I know, I was already having a relationship with God and I wasn't the least bit afraid.

God can be different things for different people. God can be simply getting outside among the trees in order to feel the power within. God for some can be better felt in a church with many people in attendance. When something brings you joy and a deep sense of peace and knowing everything will be alright, that is God. What is your definition of God?

I continued to be fascinated with God so any chance I got to go to church, I did. One time, while attending a service with one of my girl friends, the minister announced we were all going to join in a ceremony called communion. As I wasn't a member of the church, I wasn't allowed to participate. My friend went up to get her little piece of bread and wine (grape juice) and brought it back to the pew where I was sitting. She told me, before going up to get her piece of bread (which was really a cracker) and wine, she would give me some of it. She took the bread out of her mouth and gave it to me. I felt quite alienated for a few minutes that

I wasn't able to share in the grape juice. I can only imagine how we would have been able to transfer it from her to me without causing quite a stir! It went through my mind that hopefully God wouldn't care I had only a half of piece of the bread and no wine. Instinctually I felt it was okay I didn't partake in the entire ritual. I knew he wasn't mad at me. Still, I had lots of questions and wondered if it still counted as participating in communion even though I had no idea what communion was.

One day when I was playing with some of my girl friends at recess, I was teasing my best friend. I was goose stepping, my legs moving wildly out in front of me kicking up in the air when all of a sudden "Whamm!, Smack!" There was blood all over. I had kicked myself in the mouth with my knee. I dislodged a permanent tooth moving it towards the roof of my mouth. It was the same tooth the dentist had reinserted after my bike accident a few years earlier. I was rushed to the nurse's office and my dad arrived soon after. He took me to the dentist and I was told this time, they couldn't save my tooth. From that point on, I had a false tooth in place of my real one. I became acutely aware that when I said negative things, like teasing my friend, there would be consequences and a price to pay. If tooth fairies were real, there was definitely one with a contract out on my tooth. I may have escaped after the bike accident, but the fairy was not going to be denied my tooth a second time.

When I was in the 6th grade, keeping my attention focused on my school work during class was not one of my strongest traits. There were many times I would distract myself by sticking my false tooth out at a school mate named Clifford. It was great fun because he also had a false tooth and we would take turns sticking our false teeth out at each other when the teacher wasn't looking our way. Sometimes this proved to be a great distraction for other kids around us. They would see us goofing around so it would make them laugh thus bringing attention to us. More than once one of us was sent out of the classroom.

I also started hanging out with a tougher set of friends after some of my other friends started hanging out with other people. In physical education class one day, the teacher asked me to stay after class. I really didn't want to because it was recess and I wanted to play with my friends. He warned me about hanging out with a few people I had befriended. He told me I would only get in trouble if I continued to keep their company. He asked me if I was smoking. I told him "no"; although I got the sense he knew I was. Several of us girls would pile into the girls bathroom and pass around a cigarette during break time. I didn't realize he could probably smell it on me. It was more important for me to go along with my new friends than to possibly play alone at recess.

Peer pressure is real and a strong motivator of behavior. The desire and pressure to belong can also play a big part in decisions children make. A home environment, in which children feel safe and secure and enjoy a sense of belonging, can go a long way in eliminating the desire to join groups with alternate or questionable values. This can be easily overlooked as we parents have a lot of pressures of our own. We can get wrapped up in our own stress including worry over finances or personal problems or addictions and etc. As a parent, it is important to slow down, as often as possible, and pay attention to what our children may be saying. Just showing up and listening could be a key ingredient in our children's success.

I've always had many interests. One was belonging to an organization for young girls called the Campfire Girls. My mom dropped me off at a special weeklong Campfire Girl camp on her way to work during one summer vacation. I was always very nervous when I arrived each morning because I didn't know anyone. None of my friends were enrolled in the camp.

One day one of our leaders took my group for a walk through the forest looking for a place to leave a gift for the birds and squirrels. The gifts were pine cones with sunflower and other seeds on them. I remember feeling the small animals were watching us as we left the gifts. I felt they were very happy. Our leader told us we would come back in the morning to see if the forest animals left us anything. The next morning when my mom dropped me off at day camp, I was more excited than nervous. I wanted to see what the forest creatures had left us. After singing songs and having a snack, which was part of the morning ritual, our group walked along the same path as we did the day before. Overhead the forest canopy was covered by large limbs and leaves which let the sun peek through in multiple places. As we hiked along the trail, we came around a corner where we had left our gifts the day before. The area shone with glitter and shiny silvery necklaces hanging high on the branches of an old tree. Glitter sparkled on the moss covered logs and pine needles covering the forest floor. As the sun streamed through, a spider web glistened like diamonds with droplets of dew. The branches of surrounding trees were adorned in ribbons. Even the stones on the ground reflected the light of the sunshine peaking through the trees.

This was magic; and I could feel its energy throughout my entire body. I heard someone say, "The faeries have been here". From that day on, I sensed the presence of faeries, if only in very brief moments. Of course it was the Campfire leaders who created the magic in the forest that day. But nevertheless, that experience introduced me to the possibility of faeries and allowed me to begin to manifest them in my life from that day forward.

It is not advised to spread glitter or other manmade things in our forests that small animals may eat and cause injury to themselves. Faeries love for us to pick litter up instead of leaving it. By doing so, you are more apt to see one yourself.

It was during this period of my life I began spending my summers sleeping outside in a tent, rain or shine. If it was a sunny day with a clear night, I preferred to sleep underneath the stars. There was nothing like falling asleep as I stared up in the starlit sky dreaming of what must lie beyond. I always had a sense of expansiveness within my body as I lay on the earth and gazed into the heavens. I'd wake up with my sleeping bag covered in morning dew, listening to the birds singing their morning songs. I would snuggle deeper into my sleeping bag and breathe in the scent of the morning. I felt as if I was waking up in another world. I spent the summer camping in our yard surrounded by fields and trees and only going in doors to refuel on food or watch "Bewitched" and "I Dream of Jeannie" on television.

My mom worked full time as a nurse as well as being a Campfire Girls leader. Things were a bit hectic because of my mom's schedule and with the various activities associated with my belonging to the Campfire Girls. We decided that I was resourceful enough on my own and didn't really need to be part of the organization in order to have fun with my friends. I had an enterprising mind even at that age; so I was excited about starting a club with my very own name and making up my own rules.

We called it the Crazy Eight Club after my Magic Eight Ball, a toy you pose a question to, shake it up and turn it over to reveal your answer. I thought it was a great name because I was allowed to invite seven friends to join me and that made eight of us. We got together every other Thursday and did arts and craft activities. One time a lady came over and showed us how to make candles. We went on field trips to the zoo and cooked all kinds of goodies in the kitchen. We even had a camp out!

One weekend I remember quite well. We camped out in a school bus converted into a camper which belonged to one of my friend's parents. She lived way up in the forest in an area called Capitol Peak. There was forest surrounding her house for miles. We hiked, roasted marshmallows, told scary ghost stories and had a wonderful time.

My friend's dad was a logger and had his own mill right on the property so there was a giant mountain of saw dust near the barn. My friend and I got the idea of climbing this mountain of saw dust. Not wanting to get our clothes full of wood chips, we took everything off except our underwear. It turned out we were the only two out of the Crazy Eights willing to attempt the climb. It was tougher than we thought. It took us quite a while to get to the top. Just as we were nearing the top, the grownups realized what we were up to. We were told to come right down because the sawdust had lots of wooden splinters embedded in it. Since we were so close to reaching the top, we forged ahead thinking of ourselves as astronauts landing on the moon and planting the flag. We reached the top and yelled, "We made it!" as we stood there in our underwear looking proud. Our imaginary space suits held up as we slid and rolled back down the mountain of sawdust. However, I was picking splinters out of my body for the next of couple weeks.

I loved playing cards and always had a deck at hand. At night when I was in my room, I would get out my deck and play solitaire. When I got tired of playing typical card games, I would divide the cards into various stacks and stare at the cards. I would arrange, analyze and study each card as I shuffled them back together. I would even spray each card with lemon perfume. I liked my cards to smell fresh, and lemons seemed very bright. I carried my cards in my purse but I was careful about actually using this deck to play games with other people. I always had other decks for that purpose. I also slept with my deck of cards under my pillow. I had a natural affinity with the cards. Looking at the cards and expecting them to give me answers to questions seemed natural to me. It was normal to me in the same way perhaps young people today turn to the Internet for answers to their questions. At this stage of my life, I knew nothing about oracle cards, mediums or tarot. Not even on magical shows like 'Bewitched' or 'I dream of Jeannie' do I remember seeing anything about these ideas. I had no real awareness of having heard or read about ideas like oracles, past lives, reincarnation or similar metaphysical or esoteric topics.

Many times when we are young, what we pretend to be when we are playing is actually what we become as adults even if the childhood play doesn't include the full picture. Can you remember what your favorite games or activities were? How do they connect with your job or what you do now?

I always looked forward to Friday nights. The 'Brady Bunch' and the "The Partridge Family" were on the TV followed by "Love American Style". Afterwards I stayed up for the Midnight Theatre where scary movies like "Dracula" or "The Creature from the Black lagoon" would play. Elvira the witch was the hostess of the Midnight Theatre. Her humorous personality always made me laugh. But my favorite show was 'The Partridge Family'. It was about a family of musicians. My dream of being in love with a musician came from watching this show. One of the cast members, David Cassidy, sang a song called "I think I Love You". I would play my record of this song over and over again.

One time when my grandparents from Forks, Washington were spending the night, my grandma came in and asked us to turn the record player down. Playing the same song over and over again was more than she could endure even though it was all about love.

My grandparents planned on moving down to our property after my grandpa retired from logging. My mom was very excited to have them near us. The house was finished and my grandparents were scheduled to move into their new home in a week's time. It was a Friday night about 7pm. My mom was in the kitchen cleaning the dinner dishes when the phone rang. I answered the phone and it was my uncle. He asked to talk to my dad so I put the phone down so I could get my dad from outdoors. My mom asked me who it was and I told her. Before my mom got to the phone I felt a big lump in my throat. The feeling of dread enveloped me. The next thing I knew my mom let the phone drop and she was sobbing hysterically. My sister had already left to get my dad before I could move. After my dad got off the phone, we packed up and left for Forks. My grandpa had died of a heart attack. We arrived in the late night hours. The adults were in a frenzy of activity. Quickly and swiftly my mom and her siblings moved my grandma down to the new house.

I know a piece of her died that day. For many years after, she sat day in and day out in her house. Early on she had a few suitors calling on her but that subsided after numerous attempts. My grandma had fallen into a deep depression and would try to bring anyone into it if possible. It was very difficult to see her in this state and year after year her visitors dwindled. I believed my grandma wished she were dead. Unfortunately she didn't receive her wish for many years after. I call my mom a saint because she held in there and visited her when others had given up.

About this time I began noticing how alcohol played a big part in the lives of everyone around me. Advertising on television and in other media made a big deal about the appeal of alcohol. Their ads were pretty effective. It isn't surprising alcohol became a regular feature in my life as I was growing up. We kids thought it was cool to smoke and drink. On television, it seemed everyone was drinking and smoking. Even the movies geared toward family viewing, seemed to include scenes of people drinking alcohol at dinner or when entertaining company. These scenes often included domestic disputes or violence. One movie that comes to mind is

"The Parent Trap" with Haley Mills. I loved that movie and watched it many times when I was growing up. It is full of verbal fighting between the adults as well between the children. There was constant arguing going on about one thing or another.

This was the same scene playing out in my neighborhood. I witnessed parents yelling and fighting in my friends' homes as well as in my own. It was the norm. No doubt our parents had seen the same behavior in their own childhood environments.
It seemed alcohol was a normal and integral part of the world and social life I belonged to. Like many of my friends, I was introduced to alcohol at the very young age of 11. Certainly I was lucky my parents encouraged me to drink at home rather than unsupervised or at some stranger's home. I also learned as long as I wasn't driving, I could drink and it would not be a problem. Unfortunately I didn't always follow this advice.

The new school year came and the borders for school districts were changed. I was being transferred to a different school and separated from the few friends I had already made. I was devastated. I've heard it said that we make only four or five true friends in our life time. Usually these friendships develop when we are students and most open and willing to share our dreams, fears, and joys. We tend to choose friends from among our peers and fellow students.

Lacey Dawn Jackson

On the first day of middle school I felt totally alone. Even the two girls from down the street in my same grade were missing. I wanted to fit in and was willing to do most anything to make friends any way I could. One way was attending the local basketball games. Secretly I would steal alcohol from my parents' liquor cabinet and I would share it with the other kids. It probably wasn't the best way to make friends, but I made them just the same. I wanted nothing more than to belong and be accepted.

It was a typical warm and sunny summer day. I was twelve when I went to the bathroom and found I was bleeding. Months before, my mom had briefly talked to me about starting my period and gave me tampons. But I certainly wasn't prepared for the reality of it when my period came. I couldn't stop crying. I felt confused and very emotional. I got out the tampons but had trouble inserting them. That upset me even more. My poor dad came in from working in his garage and asked me why I was crying. I felt embarrassed so I told him nothing. I could tell he was frustrated because I wouldn't talk to him. I couldn't wait until my mom came home that evening. I was very stressed about using a tampon. It didn't feel right and made me want to throw up. Fortunately when my mom came home, she drove into town to the store and returned with pads for me to use instead. Soon after, it was on television news about a girl dying from Toxic Shock Syndrome, which was related to wearing a tampon too long. I felt even more uncomfortable and sensitive about the whole idea. It didn't help that at the time, and even still today, attitudes about menstruation and having periods are full of negativity. Having a period is often made equivalent to being sick or afflicted in some way. Even worse, some refer to periods as 'a woman's curse' with additional negative connotations of being dirty or contaminated. I remember people referring to "being on the rag".

I was never at ease with any of these words or concepts to describe a natural process in a woman's body each month. I tended to take the opportunity to spend more time with myself over these days if I could help it. Many times I would feign being sick or having cramps because it was what girls were taught to do. In a workshop many years later, I learned more about our menses and the emotional pains we as women may have experienced around it. In the workshop we were encouraged to see this process as something to be nurtured and honored. I wouldn't realize until many years later that I could rightfully take a few days to myself without feigning illness during my "beauty time". Luckily there are several books out now to explain this rite of passage for young girls. It isn't such a taboo subject anymore.

If you are a woman, what was your experience with menstruation like? Were you supported? Did you know what to do? What is your attitude about it today?

One of my all time favorite adventures was riding my mini-bike. We made many trails through the trees and fields and could ride for hours. My friend who lived down the street was afraid to ride a bike by herself. She often rode on the back of my bike, although, we couldn't go very fast without over-taxing the bike. One day we were riding together and like usual we were talking as we rode. All of a sudden I hit a big boulder that rolled into the path. The next thing I remember was waking up and kicking the bike off me. I was dazed and in shock.

I rolled over to stand up and found there was something wrong with my left arm. I felt very weak and my arm didn't feel right at all. I was able to get up and my friend helped me walk through the field back to my dad's garage. I told him I thought I had broken my arm. He shook his head in disbelief and told me I probably just bruised it. He helped me take off my coat and his face turned pale as he looked at my arm. We stood staring at a sharp piece of bone that had broken through the skin. He said, "Yep, I think you broke your arm."

We dropped my friend off her house as we headed into town to the clinic where my mother worked as a nurse.

The doctor set my arm and put a cast on it. However, after a few weeks, they discovered my arm wasn't healing like it should. Surgery was needed to put plates and screws into both my radius and ulna bones to enable my arm to heal straight.

This all happened a few weeks prior to going into high school. For much of that first year, I could not fully participate in P.E. classes. For the most part, I sat on the sidelines. My arm was casted for several months longer than what is usually required for a typical broken arm. Of course in truth part of the problem was I couldn't stand to be inactive and kept re-injuring my arm. I was bound and determined to continue with riding my mini bike with my one good arm. It was hard to start high school on this note. I felt crippled and impaired.

I was learning on a very physical level that trauma and breaks to our physical bodies can happen totally unexpectedly while we are engaged in what seems to be typical life. It would be years and sadly a few breaks later, before I learned that breaks on the metaphysical level appear just as suddenly. It's important to recognize these as opportunities the moment they present themselves. If the moment passes, the exact circumstances may not reappear in this life time. However we may be confronted with similar lessons in this or another lifetime.

I went to a very small high school of about 400 students. Many of the kids had known each other since grade school so it was a little challenging for me to get into the already established circles of friends. As it turned out, I made friends with other kids who were also transplants and for the most part, these are the ones who turned out to be my closest allies. I am sure if I would have been a little more self-confident with a bit more pizzazz and better looks, I could have made it into the popular crowd. Although, I do want to say, for the most part all the kids, those in the popular crowd as well as the rest, were very nice.

Just the same, high school was tough for me. I went into high school with the attitude I would rather be somewhere else. I wasn't focused on my school work at all. With my broken arm during freshman year, I could not participate in physical education and was generally feeling left out. Drinking was the norm with the kids I hung out with; and that led to using marijuana. I soon discovered I was more popular, especially with the guys, if I had extra weed on me so I started buying it in bulk. Selling it covered the costs for my own usage and gave me opportunities to interact with kids that otherwise were not in my crowd.

I wasn't ever asked for a date in high school. The times I did go to dances it was to ones where the tradition was for girls to ask guys. Most of my friends had boyfriends and went to the dances. I wanted to go too, so I would ask someone I had a crush on, buy a dress, take him out to dinner and pay for the dance and pictures. (Through personal experience, I learned exactly what guys go through when they ask a girl out, spend their hard earned money, and find out the relationship is going nowhere.) It always ended up in disaster.

I worked in town at a Dairy Queen and was able to get to know several kids from other school districts. This gave me the opportunity to party with a wider group. Although, I still hung out quite a bit with kids I had gone to grade school with before the district boundaries were changed. I was lucky in that I had a lot of girlfriends and never had a shortage of things to do with someone. It seemed all my friends were dating; but the whole process of dating and having a boyfriend continued to elude me. I desperately wanted to have a boyfriend. I was tired of feeling like the third wheel when we all went out together.

Because of my job, I needed transportation and ended up buying a dark green Plymouth Duster. My dad put specialized magnesium alloy (mag) wheels on it and I had personalized license plates with my name on them. I worked as many hours as I could during high school, so I had money to buy additional clothes, money to cruise around with, and money to buy my marijuana. True to my capitalist upbringing, I continued to buy marijuana in bulk thinking it was a great business opportunity. I figured if I was going to take the risk to buy it in the first place, I might as well make a profit. I became the gal to go to, if someone wanted to score.

This was especially true for the guys since most of my girl friends didn't smoke. The guys hung out with me all right, but unfortunately it wasn't for sex, (which I also deeply wanted because I had this notion that sex equals love). Nope, the guys hung out for the marijuana. Although it was far from ideal, it was ok with me. Attention from any guy at this time was welcomed. I felt cool. But from small things an acorn grows. This early introduction to drugs was only the beginning to my roller coaster ride and down the slippery slope that everyone talks about. Nothing at this point clued me into the darker side of the picture and lifestyle, which I was going to see firsthand in the very near future.

Preferring to spend more time dreaming by myself, I had stopped going with my parents on family camping trips. I was working at Dairy Queen more hours than what is usually considered part-time, and had a social life that didn't include hanging out with my parents and their friends. One weekend, they were camping near the Wynoochee Dam about an hour and a half drive away from home. I happily opted to stay home. I woke up Sunday morning around eight or so and noticed that it was extremely quiet. I went out on our deck and looked around. The word that came to my mind was "weird". I didn't think any more of it and was soon caught up in reading and listening to music.

The phone rang just before noon. In a voice filled with panic, my uncle asked me where my parents were. I told him they were camping. Dramatically he informed me the local volcano, Mount St. Helens, had erupted. It was unlikely my parents would be able to get home because of all the billowing ash and havoc it was causing. He told me they could be stranded where they were for several days. People were being advised driving was dangerous and to stay put. I thought, "Oh My God, the world is coming to an end and I am going to be here all by myself!" I hung up the phone and walked back outside onto the deck. "No wonder the birds were so quiet and it seemed so eerie outside" I thought to myself. The sun seemed to grow dimmer as the morning wore on, adding to my sense of doom. I think the birds were so quiet because they too were witnessing the increasing darkness and were thinking about sleep. I didn't know what to do. I turned on the television to see what was happening. I began to worry even more when I saw the chaos and paranoia on TV.

Fortunately, I wasn't scheduled to work that day, so I didn't have to think about whether or not to get into my car and drive through the ash. The mountain was about two hours by car south of where I lived and I wasn't sure what direction the ash was traveling. A couple more hours passed. It continued to grow darker outside. I really didn't know what to do. All I knew was I felt totally alone. I wished I had paid closer attention in geography class when we studied volcanoes. At least then, I might have some idea of how much longer I had to live before the lava and rock reached my house.

I had never been so glad to see my parents pull into the driveway as I was that day. As soon as they heard the mountain had blown, even though they knew they were suppose to stay right where they were, all they could think of was me at home alone. Along with several of their friends, who were also camping, they loaded up and started the long journey home. What usually was an hour and a half drive turned into a six hour drive for them. The outside of the motor home was dusty and grey. My parents were dirty and covered with ash. They had to stop every few miles or so and pour water on the windshield in order to see to drive. In the end, my dad had to replace a few things on the motor home that had been damaged by the ash, but at the time, they were glad to be stuck at home instead of stuck in the woods.

Prior to that weekend, I was tired of my parents and wished they would leave me alone so I could do whatever I wanted. After this experience, I decided I did need them around. I wasn't quite ready to be totally on my own. I wished I had remembered this when I decided to move out about a year later.

My parents insisted I live at home until I was 18 years old. The threat of losing my car and possessions kept me there. When I would announce I wanted to leave, my mom would reply by saying, "Fine! Go ahead but leave your clothes and car here!" I know their intentions were born out of love; and they appreciated more than I did, that the more mature I was before leaving, the better chance I would have of looking after myself. Nevertheless, as my 18th birthday approached, I couldn't wait to leave home.

As I sat in the chocolate shop where I was temporarily working for a neighbor, I counted the summer days waiting for another customer to come in and buy more chocolates. Between working at Dairy Queen and the Chocolate store, and partying as much as I could, the summer went by quickly. I wanted to move down to Portland, Oregon with my girlfriend from grade school. She was the one I teased right before the tooth faerie took my front tooth once and for all. She was working and going to college in Portland.

I was acutely aware of the unhappiness I was feeling. I still didn't have a boyfriend or even a date, while all my other friends were dating. I was also confused about what I was going to do in my life. I had been encouraged to start college in the fall and take computer technology courses; but I was convinced moving to Portland would be the best for me. However, after much discussion and prompting from my parents I decided to start college instead of moving to Portland.

A few days prior to my birthday, my girlfriend from Portland was up visiting her family. We decided to go out and celebrate our birthdays since hers was a few days after mine. It was a weeknight but we didn't care.

We knew we would be able to find some activity. The thing to do was to cruise in the car from one end of town to the other. Every teenager did it, especially on weekends. The cruise strip would be packed with kids.

We met up with a couple of guys we knew who had attended high school with my girlfriend. We decided to get some alcohol and have a party of our own. I was really into drinking R&R Canadian Whiskey and root beer. It was never a problem getting a fifth of booze or a 6-pack of beer. There was always someone available who would buy it for us. The last thing I remember that night was making out with one of the guys and telling him "no". I woke up at another girlfriend's house the next morning. I was sore and bruised. My underwear was on inside out and blood stained. I had been date raped. At the time I figured I deserved it because I couldn't hold my liquor and shouldn't have been making out with this guy in the first place. I shrugged it off to a few friends by saying "Well I have wanted to get laid for a long time now so my wish came true. It's just too bad I don't remember it."

It is very common for a girl who has been raped to blame herself and not report it. Because I was drunk, I figured it was my fault that it happened in the first place. If someone has been raped it is very important to call a rape relief hotline to get counseling or support.

My birthday came and went. I started college and was extremely unhappy. After a couple of weeks of classes, I found it just wasn't for me so I started skipping classes and ended up dropping out in the first quarter. I was tired of my life and I was only 18 years old. I thought the answer was to be in a relationship, live happily ever after, have children, and move into the house with the white picket fence in the front yard. It seemed it wasn't in the cards for me. This may seem a strange path for someone like me who now reads cards and channels divine messages. However, it was my path and through my experiences, I learned about spiritual gifts and how to use the ones I have been given.

BEING AN ADULT

The day came when I could no longer take it. I needed to get out and experience life. I felt like I was dying where I was. All my friends were going their separate ways and I didn't want to be left behind. I wanted to go somewhere, even if it was just anywhere. The only thing that excited me was the prospect of moving a state away, for surely then things would get better. I had yet to discover "no matter where you go, there you are!" My parents reluctantly let me go. I loaded some of my belongings into the Plymouth Duster and drove the couple of hours south to Portland to move in with my grade school girlfriend.

About a month later my dad arranged for me to have a job at the place he had worked since I was a baby. Obviously my loving parents had other ideas for me. I didn't see taking this job as in alignment with establishing my individual freedom; so much to the chagrin of my parents, I turned down the job. Instead, I got a job at a Dairy Queen in the Portland area and was quickly promoted to Assistant Manager.

I met a man who I believed to be the man of my dreams. Jake didn't have a job, was going through a divorce, and living with his grandma until he could get it all together. Best of all, he was interested in me! (I now smile at my naivety.) With Jake as my tour guide I delved deeper into the world of drugs, sex, and rock-and-roll. I was an adult, free to do whatever I pleased, and a very willing participant. (In so many ways I was more like a young floundering teenager.)

Right after meeting Jake we decided to hitchhike down to California for the fun of it. The first day we didn't get too far. We ended up in Medford, Oregon and spent the night with one of Jake's friends. The next day his friend dropped us off at the freeway where we hitched a ride with a hippie named Smokey driving a Volkswagen bus. He shared some of his marijuana with us and dropped us off outside Yreka, California. I don't remember just how far it was; but it seemed like we had been hours walking along the highway before a big car pulled over and gave us a ride. The man in the car would speak occasionally but the gal didn't say two words the whole time. It seemed as if they were at odds with each other. I also remember thinking they weren't in the habit of picking up hitchhikers. By the time they dropped us off, it was getting late and soon would be dark.

Our next ride was going as far as Mt Shasta so we decided to make that our home for the night. I was very excited because it had been a place I had always wanted to visit. What luck we were getting a ride to the exit that took us to Mt. Shasta! Once we were there we found an area far enough off the road to have some privacy where we could camp unseen for the night.
I was exhausted. Even though it got quite chilly that night, I drifted in and out of sleep not minding the hard ground beneath me. The stars twinkled brightly above the trees. I had this magical feeling of excitement and anticipation for what tomorrow would bring. We had made it to the one destination I really wanted to visit. I was enjoying this new adventure.

The next morning we stood alongside the road arguing whether or not to hitchhike into the town of Mt Shasta. I felt as if I really needed to go there but Jake wasn't interested. As we talked about what we were going to do, a car pulled over and the driver asked if we needed a ride south and whether or not we knew how to drive. I thought it was a pretty funny question but the driver explained he had been driving all night and needed a nap. Before I could say anything, Jake opened the back door and climbed in giving me his "I won" smile. I handed him my back pack and got into the front seat pouting. I was disappointed because I knew I was supposed to go visit Mt. Shasta even though I didn't know why.

The forty-something driver was named Rich. He had left Seattle the evening before and was driving to Modesto for a construction job that started the next day at 5am. He was anxious to get to Modesto to find a place to stay and get set up. He had already been in the car for about 9 hours stopping only a few times. He had also picked up someone else who drove for a few hours through the night. Rich said the guy was an awful driver, but Rich needed the sleep and said he just prayed he would wake up without a scratch and still be on the interstate closer to Modesto.

Rich and Jake made small talk while I looked out the window. I was fuming and still angry my plan hadn't worked out as intended. I was also hungry. Even though Jake sensed my feelings, he explained away my mood to Rich by saying I turned into a bear when I was hungry. I turned towards the back seat and shot Jake daggers with my eyes. As I turned back around, Rich looked at me with such kind eyes. I could tell he didn't quite know what to say but he smiled and I smiled shyly back at him.

Forty-five minutes later, we pulled into a gas station and mini mart to fill up the car. Rich looked at me and said he would buy some food for us if I would drive the rest of the way. I agreed to drive but told him I had my own money for food. This time Jake was shooting daggers at me because I had not accepted the offer of food. I was still feeling so disappointed the only memory I would have of Mt Shasta were the woods near the highway exit.

I went into the mini mart and bought a diet Pepsi and some chips. As far as I was concerned Jake could go hungry; I didn't offer to buy him anything. When I got back to the car, Rich had already been into the store, paid for the gas, bought three sandwiches, chips, and donuts. He was handing one of the sandwiches to Jake in the backseat. He offered one to me but I shook my head. He set it along with the other food between us and said I could have it later if I wanted it. Before I was even on the freeway he was snoring loudly.

As I drove I kept thinking about the sandwich but was too proud to ask Jake to unwrap it for me. A couple of hours later my stomach was really talking to me. I wanted to eat that sandwich. I was about to cave in and ask Jake to unwrap it, but as luck would have it, I spotted the sign for a rest area ahead. As we pulled in, the slowing of the car woke Rich. He looked around as I parked the car. I said, "I think we have another three hours to go". "Are you doing fine driving?" he asked me. I told him I was and that I liked to drive. After using the bathroom, I returned to the car and gobbled down the sandwich. Rich got back into the car and immediately went back to sleep, but not before he smiled approvingly when he saw me eating the sandwich.

Five hours later with one stop at the rest area, I pulled off onto the first Modesto exit. Rich thanked me for driving and handed me a ten dollar bill. "Please take this. I really appreciate you driving. You are a very good driver." I laughed, and said, I wasn't sure how he knew since he slept the whole way.

As we stood by the side of the road and watched him drive away, I kind of wished I could have stayed with him. He seemed a lot nicer than the company I was keeping at the moment. Jake and I crossed the road and went into a Skippers Fish & Chips. Jake knew I really liked fish and I realized he was trying to make up with me because I hadn't talked to him all day.

After eating, it was still early afternoon. We decided to see if we could get to at least Bakersfield before dark. As we walked to the on ramp of I-5, I was feeling pretty satisfied. My belly was full and the sun felt good against my face. I almost hoped we wouldn't get a ride right away so I could enjoy the sun. As we walked along the highway I got lost in my own world. I noticed the warm wind against my shoulders. I could smell the aroma of trees and grass.

We had been walking about 45 minutes when a Volkswagen bus pulled up. I couldn't believe my eyes. It was Smokey who had picked us up on our second day. It was as if we had met up with an old friend as we hopped in the bus. I noticed a strong smell of marijuana I hadn't noticed the other day when riding with him. As if he read my thoughts, he said he had a large shipment with him. Tossing Jake a bag, he asked him to roll a few. We arrived in Bakersfield about six hours later but in twice the time it would have normally taken. Smokey stopped at every rest area and never drove over 45 mph, which was pretty slow even for a Volkswagen. We weren't complaining as we putted down the highway in a smoke filled bus.

Our trip with Smokey came to an end well after nightfall. After roughing it for the past few nights, all I wanted was a nice hot shower and to relax. I had blisters on the bottoms of my feet and the thought of walking another step pained me. We found a cheap motel and chilled out in front of the television. We went to sleep with people arguing and yelling in the units all around us; but I was too tired to even care. I dozed off as soon as my head hit the pillow. The next morning I took my time and delayed as long as possible before Jake started nagging at me to get going. I figured we had until 11 am to check out and I was going to get every penny's worth of our stay.

We wanted to see Hollywood so we headed toward the freeway where we caught a ride to L.A. We walked around L.A. then got back on the road trying to hitch a ride to Hollywood. The first driver only took us about ten blocks then said he couldn't take us any further. On any other day, I would have thought it was because we hadn't showered, but having had a shower that morning, I knew that wasn't the reason. We shrugged it off and started walking.

I woke up that morning feeling unsettled. Partly I was upset with Jake, and partly my dream of living on the edge was turning out to be more like bad karma than nirvana. When I suggested we go to the bus station and buy tickets home to Oregon, Jake insisted on getting tickets to Sacramento instead. I caved in and we bought bus tickets to Sacramento. I ended up feeling mad at him and with myself. I had so much to learn about following what I felt inside and standing up for myself especially when it came to men. I was still caught up in pleasing others. We climbed on board and I dug my little cassette player out of my bag. I put on the ear phones and listened to the new Billy Idol tape. I listened to "White Wedding" over and over until we got to Sacramento which wasn't until the next morning.

Once in Sacramento, I was ready to hitchhike again. And besides I wanted to save our money. We walked to one of the I-5 exits heading north. The longer we walked, the more I lost my enthusiasm. It seemed no one was going to offer us a ride. After awhile, Jake suggested he would hide and I could attract a ride for the two of us. I was not happy about this strategy, but I agreed. Very soon, the driver of a semi-truck started to pull over. As soon as Jake came out of the trees, the driver took off. I knew it wasn't a good idea and refused to try it again.

It was almost dark and we hadn't seen an exit for quite some time. We had decided we would rough it again in the elements so we could save what money we had which wasn't much. After splurging on Skippers Fish & Chips once again earlier in the day, we were running quite low on funds. We had been hitching all day and had not even made it out of Sacramento. I was feeling so discouraged; and I just wanted to be home.

I was in my own little world, stewing about how bad I was feeling when a newer Lincoln Town Car with dark windows pulled over. Jake ran up to the passenger window and a guy in a suit with dark shades asked where we were going. Jake said we were headed to Portland but anywhere north would do. The business man said we could ride with him. I hurried and got into the back seat before Jake could. It felt good to sit down. I noticed all the windows were dark. It reminded me of a scene in a movie where the Mafia stops and grabs a guy from the side of the road and pressures him into giving information. In the movies, the car windows are always dark. In this case, we were certainly eager volunteers and readily got in the car. I didn't want to talk with anyone so I pretended to be asleep. The man driving introduced himself as Frank. He talked in a rough dialect while carefully picking his words as if he wanted to present himself as being more educated than was probably true. The one quick glance from his eyes showed a hardness about him. He was someone I wouldn't want as an enemy. As we pulled off the exit, I noticed he put his dark glasses back on even though it was dark.

Frank offered us his hotel room for the night. He said it was a shame to waste a good room when he was only going to be there a few hours. He checked into the hotel and came back and handed over a key. He explained he would be back really late and left. It was a nice big room with two queen-sized beds and a fancy bathroom with a huge tub. After taking a long bath and watching some television, I slept like a baby that night.

When we woke up the next morning, Frank was gone and there was a grocery bag on the table with bread and lunch meat along with bananas and orange juice. He left a note saying the goodies were for us. I was overcome with gratitude. Since then, I have often thought when people talk about how bad human nature can be, that it is just as true that human beings are capable of demonstrating spontaneous acts of kindness, like the one this man had shown us. Truly these people are angels in disguise even if we may not recognize them, or doubt it based on some of their other actions.

We got ready and headed towards the freeway. Almost immediately as we stuck out our thumbs, a big semi-truck with the Logo United States Postal Service pulled over. He was headed into McMinnville, Oregon. We had just scored a trip pretty much home. I was relieved.

When we got back, Jake and I started looking for a place to live. My girlfriend didn't want any guys living in her place so I needed to find something new. It was summer so Jake and I decided we would live in a tent at Austin Hot Springs, about an hour out of Portland. Jake had landed a job planting trees near Mt. Hood so camping at the hot springs seemed like a good idea and we didn't have to pay rent for an apartment. I had given up my job at Dairy Queen. It seemed I was taking more time off to goof around with Jake then actually working. Jake was insistent that I not work. He could keep an eye on me and my car was more available for him. During the day while Jake was at work, I read, wrote poems and stories about love and my life experiences. I sat listening to the river and lay in the sun. I loved being out in the country.

A couple of months later we decided we wanted to take another trip before winter set in. Even though the previous trip had been so chaotic, hope springs eternal for the young at heart, so off we went. Jake seemed so much happier now that he was working, so it was easy to be more optimistic about our relationship. This time we were driving my car, so it certainly could not be worse than our hitchhiking adventure. We headed towards The Dalles in Oregon, a very beautiful drive with the Columbia River on one side and water falls on the other. I felt free. I liked the idea of traveling to our heart's content.

Fast forward and we found ourselves in Las Vegas, Nevada out of money, and out of hope. Jake spent the last of our money on the gaming tables convinced he could win enough money for us to get back home. We decided we needed to get jobs to earn the money we needed. Jake convinced me stripping in a club would be one of the easiest jobs for a young girl of 18. I decided I could do it for awhile.

I walked into a club and up to the bar and told the man there I was interested in being a dancer. He came out from behind the bar and led me to a back room with lots of tiny outfits. He pulled one out and said, "Put this on and go out that door and you can strut your stuff on the stage and we will see what you got." I felt my body freeze up and thought I was going to be sick.

He left me to get changed and I sat there not knowing what to do. The only way I could leave was the same way I had come in – right past the guy behind the bar.

This whole thing didn't feel right to me and I was embarrassed and just wanted to run. For once, I listened to the little (at that moment very loud) voice inside me. Grabbing my coat, I ran out into the parking lot. I got into the car where Jake was waiting for me and said "Hurry up and Drive!" He was smiling and asked if I had just robbed them.

I was furious with myself. I couldn't believe I had let myself get to this point of even considering doing something that made me so uncomfortable. For the next few days, Jake continually reminded me that we were broke, and if I was dancing, we would have plenty of money. Secretly I was relieved I had listened to my inner voice. In the end, I asked my parents for the money we needed to get home.

When I met Jake, I knew he was buying marijuana in bulk and selling what he didn't use. I had done the same thing; so it didn't seem like such a big deal. Jake, however, dreamed of bigger and better deals. Although I knew about hard drugs like heroin and cocaine, I wasn't interested. That is, until one night when Jake came home after blowing all of our money on a large quantity of cocaine. He was ecstatic about moving into the big time. He began to tell me about all the wonderful things we were going to buy and how fabulous our life would be as soon as he could sell this batch and get this business up and running.

To celebrate, he suggested we each take a hit. In the past I had tried cocaine on occasion but never really liked it. I wasn't worried about addiction; I was above all that. I was made of stronger stuff than most people. I couldn't imagine becoming one of those washed up addicts in stairwells I had seen in downtown Portland. I knew I was strong enough to take it or leave it.

One hit, the first hit, of a hard drug can be all it takes to go down the road of addiction. Even though I thought myself above it, I easily fell victim to the intoxicating feeling of being high. Many times we will try to repeat the high of the very first time; but it is rare to experience a repeat performance. Many times people get hooked on a drug, chasing the high of that initial experience.

The drugs transported me out of our crummy apartment and into a world where I didn't have to struggle or come to terms with life and its many challenges and emotions. My life was just about chilling, until of course, the drug wore off and I was back in the reality of our crummy little apartment and my disappointing life. I was pretty much hooked on the first taste and ended up smoking all the cocaine he had for sale, in one night, while he was at work. Needless to say, Jake wasn't very happy. His new suppliers were armed with guns, knives and the know-how to ensure their business associates lived up to their promises. Explaining to the people who fronted us the drugs that we couldn't pay for it out of sales, because his girlfriend had smoked it all, was out of the question. We packed up what belongings we could carry with us in the car and skipped out in the middle of the night.

Satisfied I wouldn't smoke our supply a second time, Jake wanted to buy more cocaine. But this time he was more creative. He stole business checks from his father's briefcase and after much convincing on his part, and unsuccessful resistance on my part, I wrote out several paychecks signing his father's name. He scored his drugs and paid off the drug dealers but ended up being arrested. The police offered him a deal. The charges would be dropped if he identified the person who forged the checks. To his credit, he didn't turn me in and convinced his father to drop the charges.

After a subsequent arrest, he again refused to identify me as his partner. During this period of my life I was so afraid of being by myself and not being liked by a man, I would have done just about anything. When I think back on these times, I realize, despite the hostile and dangerous environment, I still felt protected. It is not unusual for a person in an abusive relationship to feel safe and secure and protected from having to deal with life and responsibilities on their own.

The house where we bought our supply of drugs was interesting, to say the least. One time when we walked through the front door, I looked around as we were being led to a back room. There were groups of people on different pieces of furniture and sitting on the floor. One group was engaging in sex. Another group was taking turns shooting up. Another group sat naked smoking what looked like joints.

As we sat down at the kitchen table, a man came up and asked me if I wanted to join them. The man selling the drugs must have seen the shock on my face, because he told the guy to leave me alone. He then handed over an ounce of weed and said it was for me.

He knew weed was my drug of choice. As I watched the people around me, I was drawn to watch the group of people who were shooting each other up and how one by one they would slide down the wall onto the floor or sink lower in their chairs. My body was repulsed. I felt uncomfortable but not enough to want to leave.

Another time we were led down into the basement where the manufacturing operation was taking place. As we entered, the man leading the way demanded we not look at anyone or stop and talk. As we followed him, I couldn't help but look around despite my lowered head. There were a couple of guys in lab jackets and goggles looking down onto sheets of paper. I figured they were making acid. In another corner, someone was tending to a crop of marijuana. We walked down a hallway and I wondered what was behind the closed doors. We were then led back up a flight of stairs and into a yard. I was puzzled as to why we didn't leave the way we came in. I also wondered why we didn't get what we had come for. As we got back to the car, Jake informed me he had what we had come for, and a lot more. We were going to get rid of it for them. No wonder we didn't leave out the front door.

Jake was doing a lot of business with them and was making lots of trips to the drug house. Even though the place scared me, I was also very intrigued as well as curious whenever I found out he'd been there. He kept insisting it was too dangerous for me but after much convincing, he took me with him again, and this time felt different than the other times. I could feel the stress as I walked through the door. There were women sitting on couches. Some were dressed in evening gowns and lingerie. They were talking amongst themselves. It seemed as if they were waiting for something. Everyone seemed very serious. It was as if everything was about business. The general vibe was dark.

As I sat down at the kitchen table, Jake and his dealer talked about their business. The dealer's girlfriend sat down and started talking to me. She handed me a hit of acid telling me it was some of the best. I popped it into my mouth without thinking. A few minutes later she motioned to me to follow her. She led me down a flight of stairs I hadn't seen before. At the end of a hallway she pushed on the wall to reveal a hidden room. We stepped in and I saw there were chains attached to the wall and steel contraptions lined up along one side. I had no idea what they were for. There were clothes racks full of risqué dresses and lingerie and a shelf holding all sorts of sex toys.

She handed me an outfit and asked if I wanted it. I was starting to feel the effects of the acid. I noticed Jake and the dealer had also come into the room. They were talking about the machines and how they were used. The dealer mentioned something about production going on in the room next door. I wondered what kind of production it was? (Boy! Was I naïve!)

The dealer looked at me and I felt very uncomfortable. He asked me if I wanted to be handcuffed. He laughed as I backed away from him. His girlfriend asked him to quit scaring me. She waved the lingerie at me asking if I wanted to go up to the bedroom with her and get more comfortable. My mind flashed back to an earlier discussion when Jake had mentioned she was interested in me. The room was starting to melt. I could hear lots of voices and it was as if everyone was talking about me as if I wasn't even there. I turned to Jake telling him I wanted to leave. Everyone kept telling me it wouldn't be a good idea to leave since I was frying on acid. Each of them tried convincing me to relax. They had taken acid as well and thought it would be a good idea if we all went up to a more comfortable room and chill out.

All I wanted to do at this point was to get out of there. I didn't care how high I was. Like a painting out of Dante's Inferno, I was seeing a vision of evil. I vividly recall wondering if God was punishing me for not fearing him. I knew I didn't want to get any higher at this house. I could tell Jake's dealer was upset. He cursed and said a few things to his girlfriend and she came over and tried convincing me to stay. I started walking towards a door and tried opening it but it was locked. I turned scanning the room for the door where I had entered. I was desperate to leave and started pushing on the walls. The others continued to convince me to relax and calm down but I was getting more and more determined to find my way out. They were arguing amongst themselves about what to do with me.

Finally, the girl gently grabbed my arm and led me upstairs. I was leaving with or without Jake. I rushed out of the house and got into my car. I waited for a few minutes hoping Jake had followed me. It wasn't long before he came out to the car. He wasn't very happy but I told him I didn't care and I didn't want to stay because the place was evil and I was seeing the devil.

It had started raining. I was tripping on acid and the rain made the drive just that much harder. Everything was melting. As I drove down the street, I told God I would start to fear him if it stopped me from feeling the way I was feeling. I didn't want to see the devil anymore. I saw red lights behind me and pulled the car over to the side of the road. Everything was moving so fast. In the rear window, I saw two policemen walking up to each side of the car. The next thing I know, Jake and I were walking away from the car. I looked back wondering where the policemen were.

We took a bus home that night and returned the next day to find the car. There it sat on the side of the road. I was feeling very thankful we didn't hurt anyone or get into an accident. I was feeling lucky. If we had indeed been stopped by the police, why had we not been arrested? I had recently heard something about angels and wondered if I had a guardian angel and whether my angel helped me through this situation.

I knew I had dodged a bullet by leaving the drug house and swore to myself I would never do acid again. I was feeling thankful because it so easily could have gone the other way. Jake told me the dealer and his girlfriend wanted us to join them for some sexual fun and I had ruined it by leaving. It was then I started putting two and two together and realized Jake was having a thing with the dealer's girlfriend. He didn't deny it. I felt betrayed and used. Finally it dawned on me. To Jake, I was essentially just another piece of merchandise to be traded if it meant he would gain financially from the transaction or if it would benefit him in some way. I was ready to leave. I wanted no more of it.

Soon after that, I packed my stuff in my car while Jake was at work. As I was driving off, Jake showed up and talked me into staying. Even though I wanted nothing more than to leave and move back home, it wasn't that hard for Jake to convince me to stick it out with him. I also kept thinking it would be too hard to go back home with my tail between my legs and be pegged as a failure.

It takes at least three times, and up to twenty or more times, in some cases, before a victim of abuse will leave the abuser. The abuser holds the power as they often reinforce the victim's feelings of guilt, shame, insecurity, worthlessness or worse.

One morning I woke up after another incredibly dysfunctional night. At this point, we were the only ones who knew how to freebase cocaine within the group of people who came to buy from us. So we would in turn freebase the cocaine they bought from us. Many times we ended up smoking what we had just sold right along with them. Many times I witnessed people falling onto the floor in convulsions. It turned my stomach. I would think to myself "they must really be hooked in bad".

Then one night it was my turn. The last thing I remember was taking a hit and finding myself on the floor with everyone looking down at me. They were laughing and saying I had done the funky chicken. This is what we called it when someone went into convulsions. I laughed along with them not showing them I was scared for the very last time. I had to get out.

I was aware of my growing dissatisfaction with how things were going with the drug house, the subtle and not so subtle pressure from Jake to indulge in group sex, and the way I felt when we took advantage of others to get our next hit.

A week earlier, we had skipped out of yet another apartment during the night because we were behind in the rent and knew we were going to be evicted any day.

We moved in temporarily with his grandma. One day soon after, I argued with Jake about keeping the car with me that day. After all, it was my car even though I always seemed to let him take it. I dropped him off at work telling him I wanted to go to the mall. I went back to his grandma's place and hurriedly packed my belongings before anyone returned. I left and never looked back.

LIFE BEGINS AGAIN

Thinking I was done with all the drugs, I returned to my home town and soon got a job. I was getting my life in order. I needed to get my head on straight. When I think about it now, I remember all the feelings my body experienced. My intuition was telling me to get out. I had finally listened.

About a month after leaving Jake, I got a call from his grandma asking if I knew where he was. I told her I hadn't heard from him since I left. She was crying and very upset asking me if I was lying to her. I assured her I wasn't and if I heard from Jake, I would let her know. Then I asked her why she was upset. My heart dropped when she told me she had come home from work to find her house was empty; all of her furniture was gone. Apparently Jake had sold her furniture while she was at work that day.

After moving back from Oregon and leaving the cocaine and Jake behind, I started noticing something about myself. I realized I couldn't seem to tell the simple truth. No matter what I was talking about, I would make it bigger, more expansive and fantastic, with details I was making up. I didn't like this about myself. I realized I had picked up the incredible knack of lying about everything. Later I learned cocaine is known as the lying drug. A person using cocaine starts out by hiding their drug use from others and learning to lie about it. Soon they begin to believe their own lies.

I had stopped believing and wanted to change. Something was happening within me. I had my own internal truth meter making me aware of when I was lying. It was like an alarm clock went off each time I told one. I viewed myself as superficial and imagined people could see through this veil I was hiding behind. I was like Pinocchio, the wooden puppet whose nose would grow every time he told a lie. I thought about the times I was in situations or places I didn't want to be in and wondered if God's anger of my fearlessness was creating these situations that seemed to keep occurring in my life. But now it felt less like a God who didn't want me to fear him and more like a God of love showing me how to get my life back together. When I found myself in conversations, fabricating stories or adding details that just were not true, I felt out of control. This was frustrating and yet I wasn't quite sure how to stop doing it. Time and time again I found myself lying about unimportant things and couldn't help wondering why I was even lying in the first place. I observed myself repeating the pattern over and over again and was feeling helpless.

Since I was aware of when I was lying, I boldly began to stop myself in mid- sentence anytime I started to lie about something. I changed my story to the truth even though it didn't sound as interesting and exciting as the lie would have been. There were a few times I had to literally say to the person I was talking with, "No, let me tell you how it really was." I am sure whoever was on the other side of my 'sudden change of story' thought I was crazy. A couple of times I was certainly embarrassed and felt like an idiot. I also discovered when I didn't tell the truth, the lie would stay in my mind and follow me around like a black cloud. I knew I needed to come clean with all my lies. This was very uncomfortable but I finally realized it was more uncomfortable carrying this baggage around with me all the time. As I went back to various individuals and admitted the lie, I felt the black cloud lift from me. This was very hard for me to do but I knew I needed to do it for my own sake, for my own of peace of mind. I stopped lying in a very short amount of time. I continued to lie to myself; but would not come to this realization until much later.

When I moved back to Olympia, I quickly got a job delivering x-rays and medical reports to doctors' offices in the area. I was always on call so I might make a pickup for one of the doctors, and be back in the same location a few minutes later. Some days it felt like I was just driving around in circles. But I didn't mind. The job offered lots of freedom and the flexibility to take a lunch break whenever I wanted to. It was different every day and I liked driving around. I was struggling with depression as well as trying to get Jake out of my head. And there was always the temptation to turn to cocaine as an easy out. I still couldn't kick the marijuana habit, but I was no longer interested in selling it. I wanted to be free from this monkey on my back as well.

Several months after I moved, Jake followed me to Olympia promising no drug use. He had made up with his grandma and promised her no more drugs. We got an apartment together and the very next day, he brought in big quantities of coke. It is said when you go back to an addiction, like drugs or alcohol, you pick up right where you left off. You don't go back to square one and slowly progress. I can tell you from personal experience, this is true. Within a day, I was back using huge amounts of cocaine and in as much chaos and turmoil as before. Fortunately, this relapse didn't last very long. I just couldn't take it. I really wanted to stay away from the stuff. I told Jake to leave and finally, he did.

Shortly after, I left the apartment and moved in with a girlfriend. We did typical things like go out and party every night. Since I had the freedom to go to any bar because I was actually 21, we started following different bands in town. You could say we were groupies. I was glad I had turned 21. Like many of my friends, I had been getting into clubs in the Portland area for a couple years with a fake ID, but nevertheless, I looked forward to using my real name and ID. I had used a pseudonym for so long; I actually had trouble remembering to use my real name. It proved to be a little tricky at times when I had to think twice about who I actually was when being asked for my ID.

Ever since I had hitchhiked down the I-5 corridor, I had a dream of riding a motorcycle around the U.S. I had experience as a teen with my mini bike, but my dream was the real thing. One night my girlfriend and I were at one of our regular stomping grounds waiting for the band to start, when a friend of ours who drove a motorcycle came in. I had been bugging him for a ride on his chopper for weeks. Again, I started begging him for a ride. He finally stepped down from his barstool and said, "Okay just around the block."

The chopper was a cross between a Triumph and a Harley Davidson. He had done a lot of work on it. I was very excited I was finally getting a ride. We were about half way around the block when he began to gear down as we approached the red light ahead. We were going less than 15 miles per hour when all of a sudden, an old truck hit us from the side trapping my left leg in between the truck and the bike.

I woke up semi-conscious about ten feet away from the bike. There were people above me and a paramedic was asking me questions. Everything was blurring together. I was told my pants were being cut off my leg. I asked about my red boot. I didn't want it to be cut off.

The paramedic said it was already off my foot. All I could think of was my brand new red boots. I had just purchased them that day. I had looked long and hard for a pair of red boots I liked. My attention drifted to how my body was feeling. I noticed I was shaking uncontrollably. I felt so cold. I was in the back of the ambulance heading to the hospital. I asked the medics if they had my other red boot. They assured me they had it. (I held onto my red boot for at least 5 years.)

I wanted to go to sleep but they kept poking me and asking me questions. I kept saying I was cold. I was shivering and my teeth were starting to chatter. We reached the hospital and I was rushed into the examining room. They took x-rays of my chest to check for internal bleeding and of course x-rays of my left leg. I remember hearing them say they were taking me to surgery to repair my leg. The last thing I remember was being in a room with bright lights and people above me.

When I woke up, my mom was at my side. My tibia was broken near my ankle. The femur was broken and the back ligaments of my knee were severed. The inner leg below my knee was entirely gone with only bone showing. My tail bone was also broken. What remained of my ankle was twisted and torn.

I was positioned on my back. My leg was in traction so I couldn't roll onto my side at all. I was stuck face up. They treated the extreme pain with morphine. I could anticipate the timing of the next shot so would ring the nurse's station a few minutes before it was time, knowing the nurses wouldn't get there for a while. I didn't want to take a chance of feeling my pain physically or emotionally. At one point my mom asked them to stop giving me morphine so they switched to Demerol because it isn't supposed to be as addictive. (I beg to differ!) I continued asking for it, whether I was in pain or not. The pain was very real. However, looking back, I was still going through withdrawal from cocaine and had been using my daily fix of marijuana to help. Now the marijuana had been cut off and I was looking for morphine to achieve the same result as well as take away the pain.

I dreaded the visits from the plastic surgeon who would stop by my room to trim off parts of my skin that hung off my leg. Even though I was so pumped up with pain killer, I could hear the cutting of the skin and the pressure of the cutting on my leg was enough to send me through the ceiling. There were talks and plans of future surgeries to correct my femur, knee, and leg, as well as a couple plastic surgeries to replace the skin and reshape my leg.

As I ate breakfast each day, I would carefully go through my options for meals for the following day. The ritual of filling out my food menu was something I looked forward to with anticipation. Wine was on the menu so I started circling the wine option each day. By the end of my stay I had over 30 little unopened bottles of wine in my night stand. I got used to the nurses bringing other nurses in to look at my wine collection. They would even show my wine collection to the doctors who came to check on me. I kept being asked why I didn't just drink them with my meal each night and my answer was I wanted to save the bottles and drink them all at once when I got out. I think the truth was, after opening one of the bottles, I decided it didn't taste very good so what was the use. Besides the pain medication seemed to take the edge off.

One day a girlfriend brought some weed to the hospital and we smoked it. I have to wonder why none of the staff said anything. The nurses' station wasn't that far away from my room. People must have been able to smell it. I guess it was my angels protecting me? Drug and alcohol abuse wasn't something anyone really talked much about in the 80's. There was very little education and even the media didn't focus much on use or addiction, at least not for another 10 years or so. Even though smoking was not allowed in the hospital, it seemed everyone turned a blind eye and their noses the other way.

While in the hospital, I was reading the Book of Nostradamus Prophesies written by a reputed seer who lived in the mid 1500's. I was also thinking a lot about Jesus during this time. I certainly had been saved from certain death if circumstances had been even slightly different. It was obviously not my time to go. That certainly would have been an easy out. Instead, I was spared which I believed was the Universe's way of telling me I had something I was supposed to accomplish or do. Up to this point I had taken some pretty rough roads and little did I know there would be further challenges before I really got to know myself.

The doctors advised me I would eventually have to get a knee replacement and my ankle would also have to be replaced at some point in my life. I could never ride a bike again because of the extensive severed ligaments in the back of my knee. During that initial recovery, there was discussion about fusing my ankle together but I decided against it. I started to lay my hands on my leg with the intention of healing. Even though I had a cast on my leg, I could feel the warmth radiating out from my hands and through the cast to my leg. I set the intention it was being healed. I remembered the stories I had heard and read about Jesus healing the masses and I thought if this guy could heal others, then I could heal myself as well. Besides, Jesus had mentioned a few times we could heal ourselves. He was here to help us recognize just how strong and magnificent we are.

My frame of mind at the time was fairly rebellious. I was addicted to pain medication and was pretty numbed out. I seemed to move back and forth in my spirituality in an on again, off again cycle. I was looking at five more surgeries ahead of me to correct my leg.

When I was released from the hospital I couldn't go back to my apartment because I needed someone to take care of me. I couldn't work and therefore, couldn't afford the rent on my apartment anyway. The obvious choice was to move back home. Lucky for me my mom was a nurse. Not lucky for my mom; she had just inherited the world's worst patient.

I slipped into a deep state of depression as I moved through this period of my life. I opted out of more plastic surgeries to repair my leg because the thought of another surgery made me feel ill. I was tired of someone invading my body to make it feel better. I wanted to get on with my life and wanted nothing more than to run as far away from the medical world as possible.

WHITE PICKET FENCE

I was feeling pretty lonely and depressed and I was frustrated by having to rely on others to pick me up and take me everywhere. I was used to doing things for myself. Staying at my parents was getting old very fast. I was thankful for the times my girlfriend, Tina, picked me up after she got off work and took me home with her. But even that was getting old. I didn't want to come across as a mooch.

The next man to enter my life I met at the Quarter Deck, a popular bar featuring live bands. With a cast up to my hip, I sat one evening watching my friends dance. After being rejected by my girlfriend, Matt made a bee line for me. I guess he decided to zero in on the girl with a cast who couldn't move and would have to pay attention to him. Regardless of the reason, I was happy to have the company and the attention.

When Matt came into the picture, I was glad for the distraction. Matt had an offbeat sense of humor I found engaging. He was a skilled wood worker and very good at his trade. We started hanging out together and soon I was staying at his place. It didn't take long for me to realize he had financial issues. He came home one day distraught because his vehicle had been repossessed and towed from the parking lot at work. My life was far from together so who was I to judge? They say love is blind and it seemed as if the Universe had provided me with an opportunity for a way out of this relationship.

Some years later, I realized the Universe is full of opportunities but it is always up to us to make decisions about which paths to follow. It's often not the first one we come across! This may be good advice, but here I was without a job, dealing with the reality of being disabled and feeling like I was never going to be loved again. I had outworn my welcome at home and jumped at the first opportunity that seemed to offer hope.

Soon after the car was towed, Matt and I moved closer to the warehouse where he worked since he had no transportation. Finances continued to be tight. We pinched every penny. When we discovered we could pay less income tax if we were married, we both thought it would be a good idea to get married. My immediate intuition told me not to go through with it. However, financially it made sense so we went to the justice of the peace and made it legal. I still remember the difficulty I had when it came to saying "I do".

My depression deepened. I felt like a prisoner both of my leg cast and the apartment with no view and dark and dreary weather outside. The medical bills were piling up and the truck driver's insurance company was trying to escape their liability leaving me with only one option, to bring a lawsuit against them. This wasn't in my nature but realistically I had to look at the loss of employment and the costs of projected future care of my leg, so an attorney was hired. Answering questions relating to my accident, I felt like I was on trial. I hadn't done anything but be a passenger on a bike, but I had to go through a grueling process of answering questions about the accident over and over again.

Before the accident, I was always on the go. Now I was staying home all day, in front of the television and getting more depressed. One day after getting out of bed, I was feeling particularly frustrated. I wasn't feeling good about my relationship with Matt and I was also thinking about the 1/2 inch lift the doctors were telling me I needed to use on my left shoe to help me walk easier. They said it would also help my back which had been hurting a lot. I also started to wear a special arch support in my shoe that didn't fit into just any shoe. I was finding it didn't fit most of my shoes and the only shoes it seemed to fit were what I considered to be old lady shoes.

Slowly I was coming to a depressing reality. I would not be able to wear high heeled shoes again, something I had really loved! I would especially miss my boots. I was beginning to realize I would always have a deformed and ugly leg. I wanted everything to be fixed and I was looking outside of myself for the cure.

The doctors had prescribed valium in hopes it would decrease my anxiety. Even though I didn't like the way it made me feel, I continued using it. This day the frustration and stress seemed to escalate and overwhelm me as I reached into my new bottle for my daily dose. I said, "What the hell!" and poured the entire contents into my hand. Cupping them together, I popped all of them into my mouth. There were so many, I gagged as they went down. Instantly, I realized what I had done. I started thinking about dying and it scared me. I wasn't ready to die. I stuck my finger down my throat and made myself throw up for the rest of the day. I drank salt water to encourage vomiting.

Even though I felt terribly depressed, I realized I didn't want to end my life. This actually gave me a little bit of encouragement and hope that things would get better. I realized I could end it, if I wanted to, but this was not what I wanted to do. I had to pick myself up and make this life work. I opened the phone book and found a counselor. I remember my first time sitting in her office listening to her as I wondered how someone who had not gone through what I had, could be helping someone like me? (My favorite song at the time was AC/DC's song "Highway to Hell," but for me, I had already arrived.) Talking to someone did seem to help on a very basic level.

Recent studies have suggested that speaking with anyone who will lend an ear to listen while you talk may be just as beneficial as talking with a psychologist or counselor. Maybe that's the magic, having someone to listen.

Shortly after, Matt and I moved to Detroit, Oregon to work for the summer and to help Matt's parents. The court case was in limbo and I was glad for the opportunity to go somewhere and be doing something other than staying at home and going to counseling. Matt's parents owned several businesses including a retail store, liquor store, hotel and a hamburger/pizza place. We lived in one of the hotel rooms with a kitchen.

I worked in the liquor store. Most days it was pretty quiet except for Friday when it would get busy with tourists coming in for the weekend. There were the regulars who would come in for their fifth of alcohol each Monday or even twice a week some times. I wasn't much of a drinker but found it fun to order different types of alcohol. But I think mostly, I was just glad to be working again.

Prior to moving down to Detroit, my grandpa had suffered a stroke and had been relocated to a nursing home. This brought up a lot of guilt for me. For the past several years, I had virtually ignored my grandpa as I rushed in and out of the house when I was home visiting never taking the time to stop and visit him. He was always there and I would be too caught up in my own world to even acknowledge him. Other times I hurriedly said hi. In my teenage years, the only time I would pay him any mind was when I needed extra money. I would offer to make him a pan of lasagna, for payment of course.

After his stroke, I couldn't communicate with him. He couldn't talk and much of the time was unconscious. All the times I neglected to be there with him remained in my mind as a permanent imprint. It plagued me most every day. I visited him several times after the stroke, but when he died, I was devastated. I remember crying and getting into my car driving up towards the mountain. I raced around the narrow corners with the steep drop off into the river below and the rock side of the mountain on the other side. I wanted to die. I was so heartbroken that I hadn't told him I loved him for a long time. Memories continued to haunt me. I remember him in his room at the nursing home. I went in to tell him I was moving away and I wouldn't see him as much as before. A tear rolled down the side of his face. I missed my grandpa and wished he would be standing in his doorway the next time I went home.

I continued driving crazily around each corner weaving back and forth from one side of the road to the other as

I thought about my grandpa. I remember feeling so much anger towards myself, I believed it would be a relief if a logging truck came around the corner and ran me over. It would be a relief not to feel the pain anymore. I prayed my grandfather was now in a good place. I also prayed that I would find a life down here better than I had made for myself so far.

I started to calm down when my thoughts moved towards my grandpa on my mom's side. He had passed when I was 11 years old. Years later as I contemplated this time in my life, I am sure this was an assurance from my mom's dad that he had been there to greet my other grandpa and invite him into heaven.

My mom's dad had been a logger when he lived on Earth. I am sure he also came into my thoughts to remind me I would be okay and my way of leaving the earth wasn't by way of a logging truck.

It is very important for us to be on good terms with people who are in our lives. Death comes when we least expect it. Grief more easily turns to healing after a loved one passes, when our relationships are in order and we believe we have done our best to resolve conflicts and offer kindness to those we love while they are still with us.

The summer season was over and work had slowed down in the resort town where we were living. Matt's parents no longer needed help. I was about 5 months pregnant as well. Because Matt was such a reliable worker, his former employer asked him to come back to work. We made a decision to move up to Washington.

I worked part-time at a convenience store for a little extra money and to keep from going stir crazy. I was still struggling with my inner being and noticing how unhappy I was. I had stopped smoking marijuana because of the baby, but it was still an issue as I was surrounded on a daily basis by Matt and his friends who smoked. My leg was as tender as ever. Some days I thought the pain would never go away. Considering the level of the pain, I probably would have qualified for a medical marijuana certificate by today's standards.

However, even if it had been legal, I believe that small voice within would have cautioned me this drug was wrong for me pregnant or not.

The trial was about to begin, in more ways than one. The medical bills were piling up as well as bills from debt collectors. Since the accident, several years earlier, I had been unable to pay my financial obligations. I was stressed because I felt like I was the one who had done something wrong, when all I had done was take a ride on a bike. We were not the ones at fault but nevertheless, the defense attorney's were making it seem so. It was less than a week before the trial was to begin that my attorney called to say an agreement had been reached. We were settling out of court.

After receiving the settlement, we started looking for a house to buy. I was in a hurry to purchase something of our own. Renting felt like we were throwing our money away. Besides the baby was due in a few weeks; and it would be nice to have extra rooms for the new addition. My relationship with Matt had never been a smooth one and it seemed we constantly argued. My pregnancy didn't improve things. If anything, we seemed to argue more. My mood swings certainly were not helping matters either.

My water broke about 8:30 one evening. Matt left work to take me to the hospital. He hadn't eaten and was hungry and frustrated. Right before I started to give birth, he decided to run to Burger King and grab some food. When he brought the food back into the room, I thought I was going to gag. I was feeling very frustrated by the conflict in our relationship and the constant arguments. I had yet to find peace within my heart and here I was bringing a baby into a relationship that was on the rocks no matter how we looked at it. I lacked almost any hope that I was ever going to be satisfied and happy with my life.

But in the midst of my growing level of frustration, my son arrived. Nothing had prepared me for the feeling of holding him in my arms. The love I felt for him was incredible. We decided to call him Jesse because that was the only name we could agree on.

Afterwards, I got serious about getting myself back in shape. I joined Nutri-System so I didn't have to figure out my meals and could have my food prepared for me. I started exercising every day while I cared for my bouncing baby boy. He cried much of the time in the beginning and developed jaundice at two-weeks old. He had terrible gas fits and I stayed up with him much of the night coddling him and keeping him warm. I discovered he was soothed by lying on top of the clothes dryer (not in it) as it rhythmically tumbled. I would stand half asleep next to the dryer as it hummed and gently put Jesse to sleep. In the meantime, I went back to school to finish my Administrative Assistant Certification. I wanted a better education so I could get a higher paying job.

A few months later, we found a house a few miles from where we were living. We moved in and I embraced my new job of painting, decorating and buying lots of new furnishings for the house. I was shopping a lot with the proceeds of my settlement. I paid cash for a brand new 1987 Mercury Cougar, among many other things I didn't really need. Not only had I started smoking marijuana again, I had found a new addiction. I was trying to fill a void which was more like a bottomless pit. I had become acutely aware of this empty feeling before my motorcycle accident. I wanted a car, the proverbial home with a white picket fence, and to be married. Wasn't that supposed to be the American dream? For once, I had the money to buy the things that before I could only dream about. Still something was missing.

One morning I woke up and knew I had to make some serious choices. I had a young son and if I was going to have any sort of future I had to leave behind my addiction to marijuana. I was supposed to go to school that day but decided instead to enroll in a quick fix drug rehabilitation center. The program was supposed to be a 10 day cure. I certainly could take 10 days out of my life so someone could fix me. When the baby sitter came that morning, I said good bye like usual, knowing I wasn't coming home that night. I got in the car and drove myself to the quick fix drug rehabilitation center.

Sometimes it seems like it would be easier to remain in oblivion and to continue doing the same old thing. Yet the urge to change is undeniable. Despite our best intentions, we can still make choices and decisions that seem like change but may still not be for our highest good. However, I truly believe, we make the choices to the best of our ability at the time.

While I was going through treatment, I realized I could not go back into the same environment I had shared with my husband, if I wanted to minimize temptation and focus on my recovery. Our marriage had been dead in the water for quite some time. It seemed we were just going through the motions. We had tried marital counseling but it didn't help. It was no one's fault really. We just were not a good match for each other. We were both very needy individuals when we met; I guess like attracts like. We didn't take time to get to know one another or figure out whether we really had anything in common, or shared similar lifestyles and goals. After Jesse was born, undisclosed callers phoned to tell me Matt had an affair while I was pregnant. Whether it was true or not, didn't really matter. It was the last straw and I had already given up.

I no longer had my marriage, but I did have the money I received in the settlement from my motorcycle accident. In order to temporarily stop the hurt, I continued to spend my money on needless things in order to satisfy the yearning and emptiness inside. I wanted something to fill the void.

When I left rehab, my first focus was to see my son. I was very excited. Even though it had only been a couple of weeks since I had seen him, it felt like it had been months. Spending time not being stoned and focusing on myself was energizing; and I was feeling more confident than I remember feeling in a long time.

As I pulled into the driveway of our house, it was dark. The windows were dark and there was not a single light to be seen. I had just talked to Matt earlier and he knew I was coming over to get Jesse so I was puzzled. I walked up to the door and debated whether to knock or walk in. When Matt came to visit me in rehab I told him our marriage was over. I was sure it was what I needed and wanted to do. As I reached towards the door to knock, Matt swung the door open, grabbed my arm, and pulled me into the house. He threw me up against the wall and planted his lips firmly against mine. He stuck his tongue in my mouth and I bit it. He was shocked and let me go for a moment. I ran towards the phone to call the police. Just as I dialed 911, Matt hung up the phone. He grabbed the phone cord and wrapped it around my wrists. I could hear Jesse crying in the bedroom and begged Matt to let me go to him. He told me Jesse was all right and to pay attention to him instead.

Matt said he couldn't live without me and threatened to kill me if I left him. The phone started to ring but Matt refused to answer. I was on the floor fighting him as he continued to force himself on me. He held me so tight I couldn't move. After a few minutes, someone approached the house and started shining a flashlight through one of the windows. Jesse was screaming but I could do nothing. Matt had gagged me so I could not talk or call out. The police started hammering on the door telling Matt they could see us and he needed to open the door. Finally it was as if Matt woke up and realized what he was doing. He ran to the door and opened it. One of the policemen took the gag out of my mouth and asked me if I was all right. I told him I was, and I really wanted to get to my son.

Matt was arrested that night for domestic violence. When I asked for a divorce I had not intended to live in the house since, I was the one who had initiated the separation. With Matt gone, I had the opportunity to stay there. However, I didn't feel safe and so I took Jesse and we stayed with friends until I found an apartment for the two of us. Before this night Matt, had never laid a hand on me. If anything, I had hit him several times out of frustration.

This incident was way out of character for him. Looking back on this time in my life, I can see how out of control he must have felt. I was leaving the marriage and he didn't want me to. He had done everything in his power to make me stay prior to this night, and I stuck with my decision to leave. His world was falling apart right before his eyes; and he was frustrated.

While I was in recovery, one of my friends asked if I wanted to participate in a workshop every Wednesday evening for 16 weeks. It was called PAIRS (Practical Applications of Intimate Relationship Skills). Even though I was sure I didn't want to reconcile with Matt, I did want to learn as much as I could about having a healthy relationship. I was very aware of the part I played in my relationship with Matt. I didn't blame him any more than I blamed myself for our demise.

The class was very uncomfortable at times. There were only four of us in the entire class who were single along with nine couples. Having to do some of the partner exercises with another male I didn't know very well was challenging, and made me feel vulnerable. At this point in my life it wasn't about having a relationship with anyone but myself. But before I knew it, again I was enticed and lost in the dream of having a family and living the American dream.

It seemed easier to focus attention on fixing others rather than devoting time on my own issues and fixing myself. During this time of transition, I decided I would get a tattoo of a peacock on my right breast. Peacocks represent resurrection and renewal. Since I was starting a new life and renewing my spirit, this was exactly what I needed to mark this milestone in my life. My spirit indeed may have been more than willing, but Lacey in the flesh was still very weak. Before I was willing to really work at it, my life would once again be thrown into turmoil.

Matt and I were both very angry and practiced at taking our anger out on one another. We never seemed to miss an opportunity to point a finger or try to pin the blame on each other. Unfortunately that put our son, Jesse in the middle. He was barely a year old when the custody battle began. Because of the overt displays of anger, the court decided to assign a Guardian ad Litem.

Matt and I each met with the guardian separately to determine which household would be in our son's best interest. Custody was awarded to me. Matt was not happy with the decision, and took me back to court to battle it out some more. This only fueled the fire of anger between us.

For several months after rehab, I had been able to leave marijuana behind. I reasoned the cost of forgoing pain relief in my leg was a small price to pay. I was getting my life together.

It was the contentious court case that finally removed the small bit of goodwill that remained in our relationship. Not only were we going through the custody battle, but we were fighting over the house, the cars and every bit of common property. I was incredibly unhappy with the way things were going and the never ending battle that raged month after month. Again my life seemed to be falling apart.

RUNNING AWAY FROM ME

A new man named Sam Russen entered my life. He was the distraction that would temporarily take my mind off of the day-to-day annoyances and stress. I wasn't staying connected with the rehab center, or utilizing their help and support to maintain my sobriety. I relapsed, and started smoking marijuana again, and was spending money like it was going out of style. I was in the throes of my addictive behaviors all over again. I felt out of control. So when I met this new man, my intuition nudged me to stay away but I jumped in where angels fear to tread. I was lonely, and frustrated with how everything was going in my life.

The first time I saw Sam was at a party given by a guy named Tom, who was dating Tina, one of my girlfriends from high school. Sam was sitting in the bath tub with his clothes on smoking a cigarette and holding a fifth of whiskey. There were several girls sitting on the edge of the bath tub, on the toilet and leaning up against the sink. They were all laughing together. Tom introduced Tina and me to the girls and to Sam. Sam was very likable. He was funny, witty and seemed very innocent in an odd way. Later that night, Sam and I agreed to get together for lunch the next day. He worked at a gas station as an attendant and seemed happy enough doing it. I was intrigued by his simple way of being. He lived in the moment.

The next day we took a walk to a park near his house and got something to eat at a local restaurant. We talked about our dreams and wishes. He told me he didn't have any dreams or goals. This should have been a red flag, or at least a warning sign, but I thought it was kind of nice to not be thinking about what the future may hold. I liked that he lived in the moment. The more I got to know him, the more I realized just how simple and naive he really was.

He shared his past with me, telling me he had been incarcerated for the rape of a 16 year old girl when he was in his teens. He ended up doing time until he was 18 years old. He told me about abuse he was subjected to when he was younger, which made me feel compassion towards him. When I asked him questions about the crime and about being in jail, he was upfront and honest about it. I admired him for being willing to talk about his past.

It is not unusual for abusers to gain others' trust through their willingness to talk about themselves. They can appear very genuine. In fact, many times they are genuine. It is very convincing because they do it with the utmost sincerity. It is their truth. However, in the end, often they use this trust to manipulate others.

He had lots of friends. Everyone liked Sam because he was goofy and fun. He was always happy, or at least put on a happy face. He was always positive; and that was a quality often hard to find in people. He was a great distraction from the custody battle I was having with Matt. It was nice to talk to Sam about metaphysical things and the meaning of life. He was well versed in psychology and much of the self-help stuff out there. It was the first time a man had stimulated my mind with conversation of such depth. It hadn't occurred to me at the time that in all probability, he had exposure to counselors while in prison and was very adept at talking the talk. We found we could talk for hours about anything. It was a far cry from the fighting and feeling devalued I was used to in past relationships. When I found out he had lived about an hour or more from the ocean his whole life, but had never seen the ocean, I was shocked. I took it upon myself to be the first one to take him.

It was almost New Year's Eve when Tina and I thought it would be a good idea to drive over to see the guys. Tom and Sam had moved to Pullman on the east side of the mountains to help a buddy with his pizza business.

Tina and I left right after work knowing we wouldn't get there until almost midnight. We hadn't considered the weather or thought about how treacherous the mountain passes could be if it was snowing.

As we approached the summit, we thought we were home free. We hadn't run into any bad weather. Then as we were coming down the pass into Vantage, we found ourselves in whiteout conditions. We couldn't see anything in front of us or to the side. I rolled down the window in a futile attempt to see more clearly. I couldn't see any better, but I could hear other cars and the sound of a semi-truck very near. We were inching mile by mile down the road wishing visibility was better.

Finally it started to clear up around us and we decided it was time to celebrate surviving the snow storm. We got over the Vantage Bridge and headed towards Pullman. Along the way we stopped to buy beer at a little store. We cruised down the highway with tunes cranked up.

We were listening to "The Lady Wore Black" by Queens Ryche when the car suddenly swerved over the center line and then seemingly was redirected back into our lane. We looked at each other and I slowed way down. It was as if someone intervened and set the car back on track. We slowed the car and stopped at the next exit. The snow had slowed to just a flurry here and there; but it was still very cold outside. Neither one of us said much the rest of the way. All we knew was that we were spared. Death decided to pass us by that night.

Meanwhile Matt and I were back in court for the third time fighting over our son. The court had awarded split custody of Jesse. We lived in different parts of the county. I thought it was going to be nearly impossible to work within the constraints of this arrangement, so I re-opened the custody process. Matt had started a new relationship too. I was happy he had moved on. However, the anger between us not only persisted, it escalated. This time Matt hired the lead guardian to look at our case. I was getting progressively angrier because he wouldn't let it rest but I wouldn't let it go either.

Prior to rehab, Matt and I were both what some would consider, recreational users of marijuana. I look back now and realize I went into treatment not only to deal with my drug addiction, but in hopes of finding my true essence. My soul was screaming to get noticed by me. I felt there was more to life than smoking marijuana every day and being around others who did the same.

We went back to court; and meetings with the lead guardian continued. Even though I passed my urine analysis test (UA) after confessing I had relapsed, I was ordered to continue to take future tests. Because of my relapse, my visitation rights were restricted to supervised visitation only. Matt and I were ordered to take parenting classes as well. Matt was awarded temporary custody until the guardian made her final decision. I felt betrayed because I knew I wasn't the only one using alcohol or drugs during this custody battle. But I was the only one who admittedly had undergone rehab and was now under the spotlight.

The custody battle was in full swing and I continued to meet with the Guardian Ad Litem. Sam came back from Pullman and moved in with me. In April, I found out I was pregnant with Shawn, with a due date at the end of November. The Guardian suggested Sam come in for a meeting.

Sam was very co-operative during the interview and willingly shared information about his past conviction and about the time spent in juvenile detention. Based on his history, Sam was asked to go through a psychological evaluation. The report indicated he had borderline tendencies of sexual deviancy. I was also told there was a chance he devised his answers to manipulate what he thought would achieve better results. I wasn't surprised. At this time in my life, I believed all men were sexually deviant to some degree or another. I was advised if I was going to be with Sam, he would need to go through a drug treatment program, if I was to have any chance of getting custody of Jesse.

My anger with Matt escalated. I felt like he was lying to gain momentum in our battle. He was claiming I was a bad influence on him, and that before I came into his life, he hardly ever smoked marijuana. I knew this wasn't true, but had no way to prove it. It was my word against his. Matt also brought up events in my early life. Some I had shared with him; others he learned by going through my journals while we were still together.

I was getting angrier by the day and copped an attitude with the lead guardian because Matt had searched her out; and I believed instead of being neutral, she was really on his side. In retrospect I see the situation differently and see both her actions and Matt's through a different perspective. I was blind to the fact she was only looking out for Jesse's best interest. And Matt was desperate to save his son from possible harm. I would have done the same thing, short of lying and exaggerating stories, in order to make my case. Matt was only doing what most parents would do in this situation.

The pressure was intense and I felt extremely stressed but continued to participate in weekly meetings with the guardian. Sam continued to co-operate as well. It was suggested we not live together and even limit our time together, to allow each of us to focus on our personal recovery paths. If Sam was going to be with me, he needed to participate in a drug rehabilitation program.

I decided to take an early maternity leave from my job with the state. I was feeling both stressed and depressed. Especially with the pregnancy, I just didn't have the energy to go to work. I attended as many Narcotics Anonymous (N.A.) meetings as possible, and for the first time, seriously started working the 12 steps of the program. I started asking for help and willingly received others' support. I got involved with the Activities Committee and was getting to know many great people.

In the meantime Sam had moved out and was going to an out-patient treatment program and attending N.A. meetings on a regular basis. We saw each other at the meetings. My insides were warning me of something being amiss. Things just didn't seem right; and I didn't trust him. Unfortunately I didn't slow down long enough to think about or question these intuitive warnings.

One evening Sam and I were together driving back from a meeting. As we headed towards my parents' house, I chose a back road I preferred over the busy freeway. Daylight was fading into dusk. An odd mist arose from the driver's side of the road moving across in front of us and enveloped the car. Both Sam and I were filled with a sense of heightened expectancy and physical sensitivity. It was as if we were in another time or space. We both were silent. Just then a black panther leaped across the road in front of us with the mist seeming to disappear with it. I stopped the car. I could hardly believe my eyes. I asked Sam if he saw what I saw and he said yes.

I backed up to drive down a street closest to where the panther was heading. I pulled into an area, off to the side of the road, and continued to look for signs of movement in the field in front of us. By this time it was dark, and the feeling of something supernatural happening was still in the air. We sat for some time hoping to catch a glimpse of the panther and capture the experience again, but with no luck.

I have since realized, sometimes spirit works by drawing together a confluence of natural events. When things happen simultaneously or in an unusual or odd manner, it awakens something within. Perhaps it's a psychic memory; or maybe it implants a visual image we need at that moment. It is quite different from those events we arrange in the hopes of eliciting an experience. Like for instance, when we look at the shapes of clouds, with the expectation of seeing a symbol showing up amongst them. It is a spontaneous and unusual experience that awakens and stirs something within. For me it was an arrangement of the elements that paint a picture to see and experience.

Many times I tried to talk myself into believing it never happened. For months I drove to the area of the panther sighting and slowly drove by houses to see if I could spot a big dog such as a grey hound. It was a good thing I wasn't the only one who experienced it or I might have written it off as my imagination. Needless to say, I looked into the symbolism of panther and found it is identified with freedom and empowerment. It was definitely the feeling of freedom I was fighting for at the time. I was looking to be empowered and for the confidence to continue on a positive and clean and sober path. Later I would realize a black cat might have also been the message I was repressing my psychic abilities. I was still enclosing myself in the hopes of others. I wanted to belong so badly. I had no inkling I even had psychic abilities let alone how I would utilize them.

One night Sam took me to the Space Needle in Seattle for a romantic dinner. As we waited for our desert, he knelt on one knee and proposed with an engagement ring of rubies and diamonds. My feelings of insecurity and doubt about our relationship melted into the background, at least for that night anyway.

I suspected he was seeing and sleeping with other women. The feelings of insecurity soon returned. He was in a blues band playing around town. Sitting in the crowd, I always felt as if I wasn't the only one who was there just to see Sam, not the only one taken in by his charm. I quickly realized having the ring on my finger had not really quelled my doubts or decreased my insecurity. However, I still hoped it would serve as a symbol of the seriousness of our relationship and discourage other women.

We'd been engaged only a couple of weeks when my ring disappeared from my bathroom. Sam and I were the only ones who had been in the house, and he assured me he had not taken it. Things were starting to get a bit out of hand. I didn't trust Sam and kept catching him in little lies. One day I arrived at his apartment unannounced and a young girl who lived upstairs was there. She ran out as soon as I arrived. When I asked Sam about her, he expressed dislike towards her and said she was a neighborhood nuisance. One night at a meeting, a mutual friend of ours asked if he could talk to me privately. He advised me I shouldn't trust Sam because he was up to no good. He also said I was too good for him and Sam would only lead me to heartache. I didn't have a chance to ask him any questions because Sam came up and our friend walked away. As I look back on that night, I don't believe Sam and 'our friend' were friends at all. The interaction between them that night was less than friendly. It seemed as if they had already had some words prior to that night which leads me to believe he had told Sam he disapproved of something Sam was doing.

My suspicions about Sam being unfaithful proved to be true. He was seeing the young girl he had referred to as a neighborhood nuisance. This was happening at the same time we were going to counseling, which proved to be a waste of money. Sam was playing both me and the counselor. Sam had a way of manipulating the sessions and talking about things that didn't matter until the hour was up. I remember sitting there feeling very frustrated because we weren't getting anywhere. I was hoping for a confession of some sort or a miraculous healing of some kind. Of one thing I am sure; I was devoted to finding out what made Sam tick and how I could help him instead of focusing on me. In the end I went to the counselor by myself, still in an effort to understand Sam and sexual deviancy.

And the saga continued. When I was about 7 1/2 months pregnant, Sam was arrested for suspicion of groping a 10 year old girl on school grounds. I was at home one afternoon when my mom called and asked if I had seen Sam and if I knew where he was. We were not living together and I hadn't seen him since a meeting of N.A. the day before. We had spent a short time together after the meeting, but that was all.

My mom told me the television news reported the police were on the lookout for a brown El Camino with personalized license plates in connection with possible attempted child abduction. I felt my heart sink down into my stomach. A feeling of dread ran through my body. The thought of Sam being involved was just too much to comprehend, especially with everything already happening in the custody case. Mom gave me the number they showed on television so Sam could call to clear himself.

I hung up and made a few calls to find him. Many times when I stopped at his apartment he was not there. If I asked him where he had been, he was very evasive which made me feel even more insecure about our relationship. When I reached him that day, I asked him to come over right away because I needed to talk to him about the police looking for someone who had the same kind of car as his. He arrived shortly afterwards. I told him what was going on and gave him the phone number. He willingly made the phone call; and within minutes two detectives were in my living room questioning him about the incident.

Sam told the detectives he was walking on a trail when two girls on bikes approached him. One of the girls swerved and he grabbed her to keep her from falling. One of the girls was brought to my house in the back of a police car. She identified Sam as the man who knocked her off her bike and grabbed her crotch. Sam readily agreed to go to the police station for additional questioning.

After everyone left the house, I went into the bathroom and threw up. I just wanted to die. I went into my bedroom and lay down on the bed. The phone started ringing and I knew it was my parents. I got up, picked up the phone, and told my mom Sam had been taken in for additional questioning and would be back later. I told her there had been a big misunderstanding and it would be cleared up soon.

Later that evening Sam called to tell me he had been arrested. I called my parents and they immediately came over. They asked if they could do anything for me or go to the store to get me anything to eat. Eating was the last thing I wanted to do. I just wanted to be by myself. I realized they were very concerned about me. My dad offered to drive Sam's car to their place and keep it there for the time being, just so it wasn't sitting in front of my place. I knew I ought to go to a meeting for support so I wouldn't fall into the danger zone of smoking marijuana, but I was in no condition to see anyone. Besides it was easy not to smoke because I was pregnant. I was thankful I didn't have to go to work and show my face.

Sam pleaded not guilty but was unable to meet the bail so he sat in jail. While he was in jail, two detectives came to talk to me about his past and to find out what, if anything, I knew about him. I told them all I knew and they advised me to stay away from him.

Sam called every night from jail and we talked for hours. I told him about the detectives and he said not to worry about it. Of course they would say bad things about him because of his past. I continued to ask Sam questions about things that didn't make sense to me and he came up with answers to all of it. I was lonely. I was depressed; and I was mad. I was embarrassed and ashamed to go to N.A. meetings so I became a recluse as well as becoming angrier about going through this pregnancy all by myself.

My ex-husband Matt won custody of our son Jesse which didn't appease or even curb the anger and animosity we had for one another. Matt gave me an ultimatum; either we could reconcile and live in Washington or he was going to take our son and move out of state. I could not believe he was using our son as a pawn. Ultimately they moved; and I was unable to see Jesse on a regular basis.

Coincidence or not, the decision was final and I lost custody of my oldest son the same week I gave birth to my younger son. I was angry about losing Jesse and yet elated at giving birth to Shawn. I was confused and frustrated. My heart hurt like I had never experienced pain before. I had never felt so alone. When my water broke, I was so distraught and ashamed of losing custody of Jesse, I drove myself to the hospital and didn't call anyone to tell them I was in labor. This labor was a long and drawn out one. All I kept thinking was how was I going to take care of this baby when my heart was so broken from losing another. I was angry at myself. I was angry at Matt for threatening to take Jesse out of the state if I didn't go back to him. I was angry at Sam who was in jail when I needed him the most. I gave birth to Shawn alone. I was so angry at Sam and wanted nothing to do with him because of all the things he had put me through. When filling out Shawn's birth certificate, I recorded the father as unknown.

I remember just how raw I felt inside and out. I was filled with a sense of deep abandonment and aloneness more than at any other time in my life. But I had to stay positive and functional for my newborn baby boy. Staying home was not an option; it was necessary for me to go back to work if I was going to have any quality of life for me and my boys.

I went back to my job as a clerk typist for the state and dreaded every minute of it. I was a free spirit at heart and to box me up into a regimen of 9 to 5, five days a week was a challenge. It filled me with anxiety. I still had not taken the time, or had the luxury to really find out what I wanted. I seemed to be hurrying along in my life doing what I thought everyone was supposed to be doing. I was a single parent desperately trying to make a life for me and my boys. I still looked outside of myself for answers.

Sometimes the pain is so intense we can barely function in our lives. All we want to do is find a way to numb the feelings. Since moving through these gut wrenching experiences, I have learned the importance of allowing ourselves to feel the pain. We need to do what we have to, in order to fully get in touch with our feelings. Crying, stamping our feet, hitting a pillow, and letting our bodies feel the pain will in the end help decrease it. If we continue to stuff the feelings down, and deny our pain, it continues to grow. Finding ways to release it in a healthy manner is our saving grace. And the first step is giving ourselves permission to feel the pain, no matter how horrible. Seeking a support system is important as well as finding someone to talk to who will just listen and hold the space for our healing.

I went back to N.A. meetings although I gave up my role as Activities Secretary. It was tough to go to the meetings where I empathically picked up on everyone's pain and suffering and would leave the meetings acutely aware of how desperately I still desired answers to life's bigger questions. Even though N.A. was a catalyst for learning more about myself through the 12 steps, it took a few more episodes of cocaine use to finally realize it was not something I could even be around without wanting to use it. Putting myself in the position of a cat amongst the pigeons only led to disaster.

I wanted to live the American Dream and have the support of a husband, especially now that I was raising Shawn and paying child support to Matt. I needed emotional support and the only way I could think to get it was to strive for the nuclear family, two or three kids, a white picket fence and happily ever after. Even though Matt thought he was offering this to me, I could not see life with him as consistent with my dream.

The money I had received from my settlement was just about gone. That didn't seem to matter. I was still unhappy and angry about most everything. I still didn't recognize that much of what I had been going through was the result of choices I had made. Even though I felt everyone was against me, I could have made different choices and avoided the mess I was in. But nonetheless, I was still angry and spending the last bit of my money that had been saved for future medical expenses associated with my leg injury. It wasn't even a concern at the time. When I received the settlement check several years earlier, my attorney warned me that most people spend their entire settlement the first five years of receiving it. I proved him wrong. I spent it all within the first three years.

I was getting used to the fact I could no longer see Jesse as much as I wanted. Sam was in jail and I was caring for Shawn on my own. I decided I needed more support than what I was getting through N.A. meetings. I was still questioning who God was and why I needed to fear him. I wondered if I started to fear him, "would my life get better?" I found a church in town and decided to get involved with the activities and women's group.

Unfortunately I didn't feel much of a connection with the other women. In fact they seemed very cliquish. Most of the women had husbands with good jobs, nice homes, and didn't have to work. They spent part of their free time involved in good causes, church work and activities. Our life situations couldn't have been more different. I got the impression they saw it as their mission to pick up those who had fallen to the way side and bring them to church and introduce them to Jesus.

After that it was up to the saved individual or family to miraculously transform overnight and to trust God to change their financial and home situations. The women were then free to move on to the next unfortunate creature and bring them into the fold.

I was dealing with the loss of custody of Jesse and when I shared this with someone in the group, I felt chastised. Afterwards they avoided me and I ended up avoiding them. I felt tremendous guilt and shame and felt discouraged about sharing with anyone else. It seemed they wanted nothing to do with someone who had lost custody of her child. I hadn't even mentioned all the other stuff I was going through! Later I came to understand it was probably a lack of understanding on their part. It wasn't publicized much about a woman losing custody of her children at that time. So they probably didn't know what to say. I took their avoidance and unsympathetic attitude personally but nevertheless, kept going back. That was something I learned in

Narcotics Anonymous – you keep coming back even if it feels uncomfortable. Time and time again I left the women's group gatherings feeling like I didn't belong, especially when I reached out and never got a response. Eventually, I stopped reaching out and didn't go back.

The take home message for me was the importance of giving others, who are down and out, extra love and attention. If you are in a position where you can offer support – especially to a newcomer – that should be a priority. I realize, at the time, I was judging myself more than anyone. It's important not to take others' actions personally. It is our responsibility to put ourselves in the other person's shoes so we can understand more clearly what they are going through. My self esteem was the lowest I thought it could go. Little did I know, it would sink to a new low in the not too distant future.

One person I could count on being in my life was Sam, who continued calling me almost every night from jail. When he told me everything I wanted to hear, it was easy to forget the rest. I was desperate to believe in him. I had always been one to give someone the benefit of the doubt even when my insides were telling me otherwise. It took a few more years to start believing myself, instead of believing what he wanted me to believe. He was Shawn's father; and I didn't want to screw up another relationship. I wanted nothing more than to stick it out and to make a relationship work. My parents had gone through a few challenging times and they always pulled through so I was very motivated to do the same thing.

When Shawn was almost four months old, Sam accepted a plea bargain so he wouldn't have to go to trial. He was released from jail with no place to go. He came back to my place and got a full time job at a print shop. I was still uncertain about Sam's explanation about his encounter with the girls and started to believe perhaps it was an isolated incident. Maybe the girl had bumped into him and he reacted without thinking. Was this true? Could something like this happen again? Something about his explanation never sat right with me but I had no idea it was in fact my intuition that was speaking that yes, in fact, I shouldn't believe him. Sam readily agreed to continue counseling with the sexual deviancy specialist we had been seeing before his arrest. Still, there were many things that didn't add up or make sense especially about his whereabouts throughout our relationship. It haunted me.

One night I was out of town for work and called home to check on Shawn. I called repeatedly all night long. Sam never answered the phone. I was a nervous wreck. He had promised he would be home and he knew I was going to call. When I got home, he stuck to his story about being home and not hearing the phone. It didn't sit right with me, especially knowing the number of times I called. Today I know he was lying. We continued attending N.A. meetings but I continued to feel like there was much he wasn't saying. We stopped going to counseling and I continued to be wary of his faithfulness to me.

My life was filled with worry and anxiety about the state of our relationship and over losing custody of Jesse. It started to seriously impact my work. I had used all of my sick days as maternity leave and had only recently returned to work. I felt I couldn't ask for any more time off, but I just couldn't get the gumption to leave the house. For two days I called into work and told them I couldn't make it in. The third day, I didn't bother to call. I felt so blue. When Shawn was sleeping, I found myself sitting in my chair staring out the window hoping to see a ray of light pointing to a happier future. I did this for a couple of weeks, ignoring all phone calls from my supervisor and friends. My mom stopped by to check on me bringing diapers and things for Shawn. She was worried and didn't know what to do. One day I received a letter from my employer advising me I had been dismissed for abandoning my position. I certainly could not argue the fact. I smiled as I was thinking the state department was big enough to deal with abandonment issues but who was going to help me with my feelings of abandonment?

A short time later, I was evicted from my duplex. The landlord made an excuse he wanted to do some work on the place and would need it empty for a while. We moved into another apartment down the road, and noticed someone was now living in the duplex. I look back on this and wonder if he was trying to clean up the neighborhood.

It took years for me to finally forgive myself for all the choices I had made, especially when the choices had a negative impact on my boys. I had been clueless and continued to turn a blind eye even when I knew I was bringing more shame upon myself. I wanted so much to belong and make things work that I failed to listen to that screaming voice of intuition.

One of the bravest things we can do is forgive ourselves for everything we imagine we have done to ourselves and to others, and then move on to the best of our ability. Being gentle with yourself is a good place to start. Be kind and be honest, especially with yourself. It does get easier.

My experience with the church ladies didn't crush my hope. I choose another church in Federal Way. I listened to the preacher on the radio and felt a connection with him. I really related to what he was saying, as his experiences seemed similar to my own. Let's just call them "rebel adventures" with drugs and alcohol. Sam readily agreed to go to church with me. On Sundays we drove 45 minutes to attend the church services. The preacher was very inspiring and I listened to his sermons on tape when I wasn't listening to him in church. I was feeling blessed and grateful. My little family was getting on with life and it seemed all our troubles were behind us. In truth, I went to great lengths to avoid thinking about losing custody of Jesse and obsessing about how that might not have happened, had I not been involved with Sam.

One morning I made a decision. I wanted to be "born again." Sam agreed; he wanted to be born again as well. We had been attending the church for a month and also decided we wanted to become members. We wanted to have a place of our own to worship. There was a ceremony in which we committed our lives to Jesus; and then we were led upstairs to individual rooms to talk with a church volunteer who told us what to expect. We sat down in a small room and the woman volunteer started to pray. When she was finished, she told me I was to speak in tongues so I could feel the presence of Jesus. She instructed me, saying the easiest way to open up to this phenomenon, was to just start babbling. I looked at her like she was crazy but thought to myself, "I can do this". Then and there I started speaking in tongues. I didn't feel anything but embarrassed and goofy, but when asked if I felt the spirit of God, I said "yes" because I didn't want to have to do it again. Since then I have practiced speaking in tongues and have to admit, it has brought the feeling of being in the presence of the Holy Spirit closer to me. I have also learned I can bring God, Jesus, the Holy Spirit, any guide, or angel of the light, to me just by asking, and I get the same result.

It is important to do what makes you feel the most comfortable, but at the same time, be willing to do something each day that scares you just a little bit, or a lot, depending on your goals.

It wasn't long before Sam and I stopped going to N.A. meetings and quit attending church services and activities. Despite my efforts to ignore them, disconcerting thoughts and emotions plagued me on a daily basis. I couldn't stop thinking about losing custody of Jesse; and I felt continually confused and unsure about my relationship with Sam. Eventually I was simply overwhelmed and the inevitable happened – relapse. Being sober and delving deeper into myself through church and the N.A. 12-Step Program, only made it harder for me to face myself and my situation. I went back to pot to numb my mind. I was losing myself like never before.

I've learned it's very difficult to face challenges alone or to make significant changes in my life without support. When faced with these situations, it's vital to reach out to others who can provide emotional support. The desire to withdraw and be a recluse should be a red flag warning of dangers ahead. It's time to pay attention and seek out support. The support of those close to us, like relatives and mates is important, but probably not as important as the support that can be provided by people who have faced similar challenges and successfully come out on the other side. If someone has not gone through the horrors of drug or alcohol addiction or something similar, they likely will have little awareness. Even loving family and friends can inadvertently make things worse or even enable the addiction process without understanding why or how they are doing so.

One time Sam and I were making a pot run. Driving on Interstate 5 heading north, we rounded a slight curve and suddenly came upon a two-car crash directly in front of us. The two cars were blocking both the inside lane we were in and the middle lane next to us. Even though we were driving only 55 miles an hour, it was too late to stop or to turn into the far lane to go around both cars. There was a very narrow space in between the two cars, but that was it. Realizing the desperateness of our situation, I yelled, "Oh Jesus! Help us!" The next thing I knew we were on the other side of the crash. Sam and I looked at one another in disbelief. We knew we had been spared. We joked it obviously wasn't yet our time to go. We still had things to do in this lifetime.

I started school to become a paralegal but quit. Then I signed up for beauty school and got a little further along than I had with the paralegal classes, but this too I quit. Financially, Sam and I were just getting by. He was playing in a band and was gone from home a lot of the time. It was typical for him to tell me he would be home in an hour; and five hours later he would show up. My life was in turmoil. Still, I was convinced I wanted to make this relationship work. The thought of being by myself again and raising Shawn alone scared me too much. I didn't have the confidence to believe I could make it on my own. Anytime I mentioned leaving, Sam would convince me he loved me very much and that he wouldn't know what to do without me.

What I have learned since is someone attempting to manipulate or keep others under their control will say anything to maintain their power and reach their goal.

I believe Sam did love me in his way, but I had yet to understand someone can love us and not be good for us at the same time. It seemed to be an easier task to try to fix him than to look at my own pain about losing Jesse, and raise Shawn by myself.

I landed a job packing herbs at a company close to home. It was a menial job but I really liked it because I didn't have to think about anything. One day the supervisor asked if I wanted to work overtime the next day starting at 6 in the morning. I happily jumped at the opportunity seeing it as confirmation I was doing a good job.

The evening before, Sam left in my car to go to the store saying he would come right back. Several hours passed and no Sam. He had done this before so it wasn't until much later in the evening that I began to worry. It was as if he had disappeared. Everyone I called said they hadn't seen him. He wasn't even with the guys from the band. I was very restless all night and when 6 am came and went, I was fuming about not being able to go to work. He knew I needed the car to go to work early that day. I was livid; so livid in fact I smashed his prized bass guitar into several pieces. I thought it served him right. He deserved to lose something he valued. I thought it would make me feel better; but it didn't. It only made me angrier. I was angry that he didn't think enough about me to give me a call or come home on time.

When he waltzed in the door at 7 am, I was furious. He claimed he had fallen asleep in the car. I was seeing red and started pounding on him. He ducked as I hurled pieces of his guitar towards him. He found this humorous and it enraged me even more. I continued to push him around and pound on him. He threatened to call the police but I didn't care; I was totally out of control. I continued my rampage despite his 911 call. He took every punch and held me as long as he could until I would get away. When the police arrived, I was beyond thinking. They were new targets and I flailed my arms and even kicked one of them. I was crying as they put me in the police car. Sam also started crying and begged the policemen to arrest him instead. From the back window of the car, I could see Sam standing in the driveway crying.

Sam called my parents and before I was even booked in the jail, my dad was there to bail me out. Being my first offense, they released me to my dad and I promised to show up for my designated court appearance.

In court a few weeks later, I recounted the tale of how Sam had taken my car, stayed out all night, and how I missed a work opportunity. When I told the judge about smashing the bass guitar, and beating on Sam, I added, "I would do it again in a heartbeat!" I heard laughter from others sitting in the courtroom. The judge took a deep breath and said he wouldn't advise it and maybe I shouldn't let my boyfriend borrow my car anymore. He dropped the charges on the basis it was a first offense, contingent upon my not landing back in his court again within a year. I agreed but didn't take his advice about the car. Believe it or not, a few weeks later Sam totaled my car in a crash. Now I didn't have a car at all. Things were spiraling out of control. My response was to seek a deeper and deeper level of unconsciousness, numbing myself with drugs to escape my life and situation.

Shortly after, Sam was back in jail for unpaid fines and traffic violations. Like déjà vu, we received another eviction notice. The landlord cited suspicious activities and wanted us gone. While Sam was in jail, some of his friends and band members moved our belongings up to Lakewood, where we could live with a couple of his band members in a big house with plenty of extra room. The house was situated in the midst of an area with gangs, drug abusers, sex offenders and generally people making dubious choices in their lives. There were efforts by the residents to clean it up, but it was considered a "bad part of town" and flagged as a neighborhood most people would not want to visit in the middle of the night, if at all.

The house was off the road about 60 yards, with a long circular driveway with trees and mowed lawn in the middle. On each side of the house were trees and a chain link fence almost completely covered by indistinguishable shrubs and plants. The band's practice room was called "the Sanctuary" and was located behind the house and across the small little back yard. It was a garage, almost taken over by black berry bushes on the outside walls. An apartment building stood to the side on the other side of the fence. Directly behind the garage stood a fence completely covered and overgrown with blackberry vines, with more apartment buildings on the other side. Our house remained virtually invisible to all others around.

I looked forward to the new start. I fell prey to the deception of the "geographical cure" – things would get much better by changing towns and scenery. We could start anew. I had yet to learn it was me that had to change from the inside. By moving we were only taking our problems with us.

Shortly after the move, Sam was released from jail and went back to his job at the print shop. His boss recognized Sam as experienced and good at his job. Despite his faults, Sam was a perfectionist whether he was typesetting a business card or cleaning the house. (When he cleaned, he cleaned!) Once I caught him in the bathroom scrubbing the floor with a toothbrush. When we were together, Sam always did the housecleaning. He was also generous to a fault. It was not unusual for him to give his money away or spend it frivolously. He spent more money on drugs than on rent. I made it a point to get to him as soon as he got paid, in order to make sure I could get my hands on the money for our living expenses.

I felt very insecure around the band's groupies. My intuition was guiding me but I didn't listen. Despite the mounting evidence of Sam's infidelities and dysfunction,

I needed real proof and not just a gut feeling. I continued looking for something more concrete that would prove he was cheating, but the evidence eluded me.

Now, I see myself in my clients dealing with similar relationships and situations. They are looking for the final piece of the puzzle, that last piece of concrete evidence to prove their husband or partner is cheating. In reality the picture is already complete and they don't really need anything but what is already before their eyes. My job as a psychic is as much to reveal what is in the spirit world as to show them what they can clearly see in front of them and to help them accept or confront what they can already see or feel.

I felt as if everyone knew something that was being kept secret from me. I convinced myself I was just being paranoid; it was all in my imagination. I didn't realize at the time that often our imagination is actually our intuition communicating with us. I continued to feel more and more uncomfortable in my relationship but instead of trusting myself, I longed for someone else to explain things to me. I voiced my concerns but no one came forward or wanted to get involved. Sam continually assured me "nothing is going on".

I worked very hard to make ends meet. I have always been very enterprising and dedicated to making sure I had the money to support myself and my two boys. I was paying child support to Matt. My parents pitched in buying Jesse clothes and other things he needed. It frustrates me, even today when I hear of men and women who blow off their responsibilities in this regard, many of whom are in much better economic circumstances than I was at the time.

When I didn't have a job or was working only part time, I brought in extra money by selling my blood plasma. I would show up at the plasma center a couple times a week even though it left me feeling weak. I thought to myself, "at least there will be food on the table", and prayed it would be high in iron! Each time I walked into the center I could feel the resistance in my body. On the morning of the days I planned to donate, I got a head ache that would last until the next day. Afterwards, I usually didn't do much other than numb myself with food and television. I would sit in the waiting room of the Plasma Center observing the different types of people. Some lived on the street. Others were in work clothes coming in during their lunch hour. There were people of all ages and races. I could see their auras and noticed most of them were unhealthy and drained of energy, much like me. I always smiled and made eye contact with anyone that would make eye contact with me. Everyone needed a smile; and it made me feel better when someone smiled back.

The nurses pricked my finger to see if I was okay to give plasma. They checked for hard drugs as well as levels of iron. There were a couple times I was turned away because of low iron. Most of the people giving plasma either smoked cigarettes or weed and drank alcohol excessively, or all the above. I wondered how the plasma we were selling could be healthy for someone needing the transfusion to save their life. My body resisted the needle every time. I felt like I didn't belong there; and yet I didn't see another way to get the money or to find my way out of my current situation.

I started working at a popular rock-n-roll night club down the street from where we lived. As a hostess at the door, I greeted people and checked IDs. I loved the job. It was a lively dance club with regular customers; and I loved working at a place where people were in happy moods. I got to dress up and always received lots of compliments. This did wonders for my self esteem.

I became friends with a number of other employees. That's how I got to know Liam and his girl friend, Sharon. She lived out of town, but Liam lived less than a block away from us, and would often stop over and visit. We liked to play backgammon. There were many times Sam would come up and tell him in a very deep voice, "She's mine". I was very embarrassed at the time. It seemed the more confident I became, the more Sam wanted to control me. I never stopped doubting my relationship with him because I believed he wasn't being honest with me.

The guys in the band were spending more time practicing and Sam was becoming more and more irresponsible. There seemed to be more drugs flowing on party nights which started to take place almost every night of the week. I wondered, had the number of parties increased or was I just waking up to the true nature of our environment? When I'd come home from work, there were always at least a few people at the house. Often Shawn and another little boy, the son of another member of the house, would play unattended by themselves in the house while the guys were out in the sanctuary. I dreaded going to work because I didn't think Shawn was really be being watched or cared for.

It was so chaotic at the house and since I worked weekends at the nightclub, Shawn spent most weekends with my parents. The weekends I had Jesse for visitation, all three of us, the two boys and I, spent at my parents' home.

The day of my 30th birthday, my parents agreed to take Shawn for a few days. That night, the guys had a big bash for me. There were several bands and lots of people. The night club was right down the street and many people spilled over to our place after hours to jam and party. People I knew from the night club came up to say "hi". Every time a guy talked to me, Sam would appear out of nowhere and tell them I was his woman and he was watching them. I found it interesting whenever I wanted to find Sam at a party, he was forever missing and no one seemed to know his whereabouts. That is, until I talked to another guy; then Sam would magically reappear.

Sam's behavior clearly was intimidating and the guys were so uncomfortable they ignored me for the rest of the night. He was clearly jealous even though I gave him no reason to be. I also felt so insecure because there were strippers coming over to the house and I was sure Sam was sleeping with one of them. In his mind, I was his property to have when he wanted me, but in the meantime, no one else was to have any access, not even for conversation.

The night of my party, I wanted to escape and headed for my bedroom. Inside I found several girls, including a couple of the strippers, sitting on my bed snorting cocaine. The temptation was too much and I joined them, but in the end I felt worse.

I was being eaten alive by my doubts and suspicions about my relationship with Sam. For the first time, I was noticing just how trapped I really felt. Even though I could have walked right out the door and never looked back, it was as though an energetic force was holding me prisoner. I had been with Sam for four years. Apart from the incident with the 10-year girl over a year ago, it had not been all bad. He treated Shawn well, for the most part, and my parents liked him. My grandma had a special spot in her heart for Sam and always said so whenever she got the chance. Sam helped her with many projects around her house such as replacing the roof and doing some painting. She always enjoyed making him lunch and visiting with him.

Sam was a hard worker but also a hard player. We had gone through a lot together and shared our lives with each other. However, I tended to hold back a bit, as he tended to use information I shared with him against me. Nevertheless, I was hooked.

Little did I know he was in fact using everything I shared with him in an energetic and yet subtle manner. It's not unusual for someone to exert a stronger influence on an energetic and emotional level than on a physical and verbal level.

I was beginning to sense there was something better out there for me. A few of my friends expressed concern about my relationship with Sam. A couple of girlfriends stopped hanging around because of the vibe they kept getting from him. Years later, they both told me they were afraid of him; and the way he treated me was awful. They both sensed Sam didn't want them around. They didn't know how to tell me that Sam was chasing them away; instead they just disappeared. In truth, I probably wouldn't have listened to them or believed them.

Women in abusive relationships often have at least one loved one or friend voice concern about the relationship. It is very important to take heed and listen, especially if the message is one you keep hearing from different people. How others act around you can also be a sign. Be advised, if your friends and family stop coming around or contacting you, it's time to pay attention.

Chances are they are afraid to express what they are feeling or observing and they may even think you won't listen, which is quite often the case.

I no longer wanted to be a prisoner. I felt hopeful and had more self-confidence than I had in a long while. I was committed to keeping this feeling alive. I realized my dreams and aspirations didn't include Sam anymore. But before I was ready to take action, in the meantime I pursued some of my interests. From a very early age, I have always loved to read and write. I used to put pages of paper together, make a cover out of card board and bind a book together. I wrote little short stories in them. I decided to combine my love of writing and my love of cooking and creating fine foods together by compiling a recipe book. I took a self-publishing workshop at a community college that motivated and inspired me. I asked relatives for their favorite recipes and assembled them into a book. I had several books printed and sold them. It was a lot of fun and infused me with a sense of satisfaction. It prompted me to get more into my writing which I had given up several years earlier when my ex-husband Matt read my journals and mined them for material to use against me in court.

I left the night club. It was easier that way. I was able to ensure Shawn's care and safety while the guys practiced and partied in the Sanctuary. Sam's drug intake had grown exponentially worse. It was getting so far out of control even one of our roommates complained about all the partying and suggested Sam needed to settle down. Sam was spending his entire paycheck on marijuana. He would buy an ounce thinking he would sell it, but inevitably he smoked it and gave it away. I saw him going steadily downhill.

My friend Liam told me I needed to leave Sam saying he was no good for me and I deserved better. Liam never came back to the house after that conversation. I stopped by his house a few times when his girlfriend was visiting, but he was careful not to say much to me. In retrospect, I believe Sam told him not to come by and visit me anymore. Sam didn't want me to have any male friends; and he also didn't want me having any friends with ideas he didn't like. And it wasn't too different with my girlfriends. Even though he did not tell me directly not to associate with them, he singled out a few and made it clear he didn't approve of them by saying negative things about them.

Christmas was coming and I knew I had to get some sort of part-time job. I had been working temporary administration office jobs but decided I really didn't like sitting at a desk all day. I landed a job at a retail clothing store down the street.

I had never worked at a clothing store before but I knew it would be easy. After all, I got to dress up, smile at the customers and help them find what they needed. One day a woman came into the store and was browsing with a purpose. I greeted her and asked if she needed help with anything. We talked about general stuff, about the clothes I was selling and how I liked working for the company. She asked me about my working experience. I told her I had completed a two-year Administrative Assistant certification program and had experience with various office jobs. I explained I didn't like sitting at a desk all day, but would love an administrative job that included lots of variety.

I didn't realize at the time I was speaking with Tammy, the regional manager of the clothing store. Later my store manager told me Tammy really liked me and was impressed with my customer service skills as well as my confidence in my job. A few days later the store manager asked if I would be interested in interviewing for a position the company was creating. The corporate office was located on the East Coast with regional managers located throughout the country. The regional managers traveled to various retail stores working with the management teams to ensure sales success in the districts as well as in the entire region. The position I would be applying for was for a regional assistant, acting as a liaison between the corporate office and district offices, as well as all the retail stores in the region. There would be lots of variety.

The position would be headquartered about 45 minutes north of where I currently lived but I didn't care. I was in a volatile environment and was looking for any place new. I still hadn't found a place to live on my own, nor did I have the finances to afford one. I was feeling stuck but also confident something would open up for me pretty soon. I was ready and open to receive whatever opportunity came along.

Most nights Sam stayed out in the band room. Our relationship was all but over. I was biding my time until I could pull together enough money to get a place of my own. The energy around me felt dark and evil and I had to find a way out.

The guys in the band were playing heavy metal music that frankly sounded awful. I no longer fit into this world. The band was looking for a singer; and a guy from California, who had just moved up to the area, answered their advertisement. As soon as Jim opened his mouth and started singing, everyone in the room was blown away. He was definitely in a league of his own. His talent and experience far exceeded that of the other band members. He was very confident and knew exactly what he was looking for in a group. His audition was more about him interviewing the guys than the other way around.

Jim decided he would give the guys a try but not before making it clear he wanted some changes. They got rid of one of the guitar players and started playing a more rock-n-roll Jimmy Page kind of sound. The band sounded great. They quickly got gigs throughout the Seattle/Tacoma area and recorded some tracks in a studio.

My life was changing, not necessarily due to Jim and the band, but because of a new person in my life, Jim's girlfriend, Hope. She was a beautiful blond hippie surfer chick. Hope was independent and didn't hold back in telling it like it was. She had a voice and she had the confidence to back it up. She had a daughter the same age as Shawn. She was an avid reader, and introduced me to all kinds of new and interesting books on Native American spirituality and Earth Magic. Hope was also into drumming circles and invited me to attend with her. She opened an entirely new world for me. I felt more alive than I had in years. Her name said it all; Hope had entered my life.

While visiting my parents, I spotted a flyer stapled to a telephone pole advertising Tuesday night meetings to practice shamanistic techniques led by a shaman named Spirit Wolf. Something inside me lit up. I grew even more excited when I called the number and found out the meetings were held a couple of miles from my parents' house. This was ideal as Shawn could be with my parents while I attended the gatherings. Spirit Wolf was a Native American woman with very long black hair with a grey streak of hair running down the side of her face. Her hair was often braided, sometimes with a feather. She was tall and very lean; and wore moccasin boots over her tight fitting jeans.

When I went to my first meeting, I was greeted outside by an older woman with grey hair and kind but discerning eyes. She was leaning over a bush full of red and pink flower buds just beginning to bloom. "See the faeries?" She whispered over the flowers. At first I thought she was kidding, but she waved me closer. Kneeling down over the flowers and squinting my eyes, I did indeed see something. It must have been a fly or another insect I thought to myself. She whispered, "Look closely dear, they're all over." I followed her into the house where several people were gathered waiting for the event to begin. When Spirit Wolf entered the room, everyone got quiet and took their seats. She started by mentioning how the faeries were out in force that afternoon and especially since it had been raining, they were happy to be among the flowers drinking the rain droplets from the blooms. She could see the spirit guides and angels around us serving as our protectors. She talked about white light and the importance of surrounding ourselves with it.

Spirit Wolf explained we were going to practice seeing guides around each other. Using white paper as a back drop against a wall, we took turns standing in front of the papered wall while others watched and took notes of what they saw. Afterwards we shared our impressions and were quite surprised to realize, most of the time, two or more people reported seeing the same thing around the person standing in front of the white paper. I was amazed and very excited about what I was learning. It felt very natural and seemed to get easier each time a new person stood up and I viewed them against the white paper. "This is fun!" I thought. It all seemed so familiar. I couldn't wait until the next week.

During the next several weeks, Spirit Wolf led us through a variety of exercises and techniques to get us in touch with our ability to see and communicate with our guides and angels. Although I was thrilled with what I was learning, I tended to be somewhat aloof and held myself somewhat apart from the group making no real attempt to get to know the others. I noticed I was withdrawn and quieter than usual. The need to expend increasing amounts of energy, to just hold it together in my living environment, was draining my energy and taking its toll. It felt good to be out from under Sam's controlling grasp. And yet at the same time, it seems I had forgotten how to be me. At break time, I would scurry outside and practice seeing the faeries so no one would engage me in conversation or ask questions I didn't want to answer about my life. Interestingly enough, Sam and the guys called their band practice room "the Sanctuary". Here in this place, I was finding my own sanctuary outside of the one in the backyard of the place I still called home.

After each meeting, I always hurried to leave, thinking my motivation was to get back to Shawn. As I reflect on this many years later, I realize I was hiding myself; I didn't want anyone to get too close. One night as everyone was leaving, Spirit Wolf asked me to stay, saying she wanted to talk. The room emptied except for the older woman who owned the home and who had pointed out the faeries on that first night. Spirit Wolf briefly spoke to the woman who looked over at me smiling and said, "I will see you later." She left the room closing the door behind her.

Spirit Wolf was quiet for a few moments and I was beginning to get a little nervous. Thoughts started flying through my mind, including "Was she going to ask me not to come anymore?" She started to speak. "You have a guide that has been very adamant about me talking to you. He is very strong-willed and insistent. He is powerful and here to help you at this time in your life. He will only stay for a time but will come back later throughout your life. He appears as a very large Native American man. His name is Wind Maker."

As she said his name, a breeze flowed through the room. I had goose bumps and felt a powerful presence come up behind me, stopping just short of my body. I looked back over my shoulder and didn't see anyone. Spirit Wolf continued, "He is here to give you an etheric gift". I didn't understand what this meant but I didn't say anything and continued to listen. "Wind Maker is placing a necklace around your neck. This necklace is very beautiful. It is an arrowhead made of turquoise.

You are to wear it to represent the power you have within and to remind you that all you have to do is ask for help." I wanted to cry. I felt a strange connection that was familiar, yet so foreign to me. Holding back my tears I said, "I feel so honored; tell him I feel very honored." Spirit Wolf laughed, "He hears you". You can talk directly to him in your mind or out loud. He is here for you".

I thanked Spirit Wolf and I started to leave. She put her hand on my arm to stop me. "He also wants me to tell you, where you are living is very dangerous. You must leave very soon." Another jolt ran through my body; and tears streamed down my face. I felt very exposed and vulnerable. I had learned to hide my fears and present a very strong front. Now, I had no place to hide. How did

Spirit Wolf know anything about me? I wondered. What would make her say such a thing? I had not shared anything about the hell I was living. To have her tell me I was in danger was startling. Even though I had been feeling so unsettled and discontent prior to this evening, I was still denying my intuition which was calling out to me to leave my current situation. Now it had been said out loud and confirmed by a guide who called himself Wind Maker, and a woman named Spirit Wolf. My mind was reeling.

After my talk with Spirit Wolf I went to my parents' house to get Shawn. My mom informed me she had talked to Matt and made arrangements to pick up Jesse for the weekend. I told my parents that Shawn and I would join them on the weekend when Jesse was there and we headed home. As I drove into the driveway, a familiar feeling of dread enveloped me. For a Tuesday night band practice, there seem to be a lot of parked cars.

It was late and Shawn and I needed to get to bed. It would be an early morning for the both of us. I got him ready for bed but he wasn't happy about it. He was picking up on the bad vibrations running through the house. I tucked him into his top bunk and went out to the Sanctuary. I could smell marijuana when I walked in the door. I told the guys they needed to wrap it up, explaining I wanted to go to bed and I was sure the neighbors wanted to go to sleep as well. The guys responded with looks with daggers in them, but I felt them bounce right off. I didn't care who liked me or not. As I stepped outside, the music started back up. I popped my head back in and one of the guys promised, "We are almost done."

They had a fire burning in the back yard and I stopped to warm myself, feeling the heat throughout my body. I breathed the fresh air as I listened to the wind blowing through the trees. The rustling of the leaves was soothing. It was as if they were telling me all would be well. I looked up at the moon. She had been my savior of late. I felt safe when I connected to her. I felt a wholeness deep within and I wanted more of that feeling.

My mind drifted to my friend Hope. I missed seeing her. She was one of the only rational and responsible gals that hung around this group. Thinking of her, I realized how much I had to be thankful for. She had introduced me to so many ideas and literally opened my life to new possibilities. She was always positive and stood up for herself. She didn't care what others thought of her and I admired that strength. But lately, she hardly ever came around. She and Jim had decided to move back to California. There was a shift in the air. She was feeling it too. I had become acutely aware I didn't feel good in these surroundings. I was waking up to many questions I couldn't answer. I was questioning my youthful dream of living with a musician and experiencing a kind of wild life I imagined.

I was beginning to think I had watched too many Partridge Family shows and maybe it wasn't very realistic. Besides, dreams were supposed to feel good, and this dream I was living wasn't feeling good at all. I had been running away from the pain of losing custody of Jesse and feeling an inner ache of not having both my boys with me. The only time I remember feeling anything close to happiness was when Jesse joined us for the summer holidays and he and Shawn spent hours playing together on those hot summer days.

Without Jim, the band was sounding worse. The guys finished playing and came out of the garage interrupting my communion with the moon, which was quickly forgotten. I was tired and I wanted to go to bed but the guys weren't leaving. They were just hanging around. I stood in front of the fire looking up at the moon reflecting on the conversation with Wind Maker. Usually, I was excited to share with the guys the techniques I learned at my meetings with Spirit Wolf. That night, I was hoping no one would ask. I couldn't get her words out of my mind. I was on edge, even more than usual and kept hearing the words "Get out of here!"

Instead of leaving, the guys were intent on partying; more wood was put on the fire. "Leave!" I heard ring in my ears. The word echoed in my mind. I wondered if it was my inner voice demanding the guys to leave, or was it the voice of Wind Maker, my guide, instructing me to leave? I didn't belong here any longer but I had no idea where I would go. I walked into the house, lifted my son out of bed and drove away in the car. After a short time, I realized I didn't have very much gas and needed to make a decision. I stopped at a pay phone and called a gal who came by the house occasionally. She was somewhat of a gypsy and wanderer who liked to hang out with the musicians. I knew she was staying at a guy's house not far from where we were parked. I was thankful when I heard her voice and she said we could stay the night. It was a restless night. My mind was full of thoughts of how Matt had punished me for leaving him by wrestling Jesse away from me. These thoughts played in never ending loops through my mind.

AWAKENING TO MY OWN NEEDS

I accepted the job as regional assistant at the clothing store and re-located Shawn to a daycare near my parents. We could stay with them until I got things sorted out. The commute to work was an hour and a half and I was trying to save every penny to get a place of my own. Occasionally I stayed with Sam to avoid the long commute and gas expense. Not too surprisingly, things with Sam just seemed to get worse. There were even more parties; and more people I didn't know, hung out at the house. I kept telling myself it was okay to be there and was worth it to save the money on gas and the commute time to work. I was growing braver and more confident. I wasn't afraid to stand up for myself and speak my mind, which clearly annoyed Sam. No longer was I content to sit back and watch him implode.

He insisted I come back. I told him this would only be possible if he would quit fooling around with other women and being deceptive about his activities. He adamantly denied my allegations and suggested they were all part of my over-active imagination. I wanted to trust what he was telling me, but my insides were screaming at me, "Don't believe it." The tension and conflict escalated. I so wanted him to see what seemed so obvious to me. As usual, he was adept at skirting around the truth, careful to not say one way or another, what he was really up to. This frustrated me even more. I had always given people the benefit of the doubt, but my intuition was waking up and it was getting harder and harder to believe him. I wanted him to tell me straight out and admit that my suspicions were true. I was trying to control him and the environment and was finally realizing it was useless. The effort was weighing on me like a ton of bricks.

It was a very warm spring morning and the first day of my new job as regional assistant. Sam and I were fighting and I had mouthed off one too many times pushing him to the edge. I was speaking my mind loud and clear and he didn't like it. I wanted to know the truth. My intuition was screaming out he was fooling around with another musician who was staying in the house with one of our roommates. That morning he called in sick to work and the woman I suspected of being his lover was also in the house. I couldn't take it any longer.

This was crunch time and I needed a commitment from him that he was going to change. I wanted a new life with him along with my new job. I wanted him to admit he was fooling around and agree to stop. He continued to deny my accusations and was getting angrier by the minute, but that didn't stop me. I continued to verbally push him. The next thing I knew, he was strangling me. He had been violent with me one other time when he slapped me in the jaw after I pushed him for more information. After that incident, I believed his explanation and excuse and let it go. But now, his hands were around my throat and I desperately kept trying to grab his hands to break his grasp. He was lost in the moment and shaking me. Despite my struggle, things around me started to go black. I struggled more. All of a sudden, he seemed to snap out of it and starting hugging me. He squeezed me, rocking me back and forth telling me he was sorry over and over again. I was livid.

All I wanted to do was run as far away as I could. I knew I had to get my wits about me. It was my first day at a job I believed was my ticket out of the hell I was living. The past few days had been very hot and I couldn't imagine wearing something as warm as a turtle neck the first day of this very important job. But I did wear one, to hide the impression of his fingers that now showed as red and purple in perfect formation on each side of my neck. As I drove to work that morning, I wondered why no one in the house had come to my rescue. I knew they must have heard us. I passed it off blaming myself for having provoked him. I suppose it really wasn't their business. I also remembered how Sam tended to control his environment especially when it involved me. Others feared Sam even if they didn't want to admit it.

Although for the most part I was living with my parents, I still occasionally made futile attempts to resurrect the relationship with Sam and would spend nights at the Sanctuary. It took me six months to get the gumption and willpower to leave him and the situation for good. My intention was to eventually find a place of my own closer to my job. The drive from my parent's house to work took about an hour and a half, so I moved Shawn to a daycare closer to work so we could spend that commuting time together every day.

Nothing had really changed at the Sanctuary. Shawn and I were planning to spend the night, but the noise and partying were more than I could stand. The guys practiced late into the night and people were partying in the Sanctuary band room as Shawn and I were in the house getting ready for bed. For the millionth time, I had had it!

It's not unusual for victims of domestic abuse and violence to make repeated excuses for not leaving a dangerous situation. This is especially true as they are usually under the influence of a person who convincingly usurps their sense of power. Although it varies from one person to another, it has been estimated a victim of domestic abuse tries to leave at least a dozen times before actually doing so.

I packed more of our belongings, loaded them and Shawn into the car, and drove away. I knew then we couldn't go back but I didn't know where to go. I had no money and didn't want to bother anyone. My parents lived 45 minutes away and in the opposite direction I needed to drive to work in the morning. Without a plan, I simply got on the highway and started driving in the direction of my job. I figured wherever we ended up, at least I would be closer to work. I exited the highway and turned into a marina parking lot that looked like a safe place to spend the night. There were other parked cars probably belonging to people living on the boats.

I wrapped Shawn so he was cozy and we slept – me with one eye open the whole night. I wasn't afraid of sleeping in the car but was anxious about finding a place for us to live. I was living payday to payday and spending a lot of money on gas for the long commute. At one point during the night, I opened my eyes and there was the moon shining into my face. There was something about the full moon that made me feel strong. I knew I had made the right decision, although I was totally unsure of my next steps. I knew I could turn to my parents but I also knew they could not identify with, or really understand, the reality of my life. I could not expect them to. They were big believers in sticking it out and moving through the tough times in relationships together. They had successfully navigated their difficult times. But my dad was a much different person than Sam.

The problems we were facing were far more difficult than anything my parents had experienced in their marriage. There was another reason not to stay with my parents; if Sam came looking for me, their house was the first place he would look. I wanted to find a place where no one knew me, and I didn't want to leave a trail for Sam. I needed to find a safe place for me and Shawn to start a life of our own.

During this time I was using a deck of animal totem oracle cards. These were my first cards and they continued to be very important in guiding me and helping me find serenity in my new life. I looked at them as messengers of God.

There are many tools that help us get through life's challenges. Some people may read the bible or even read random bible passages like an oracle. To this day, the animal totem cards continue to be a huge support to me, especially when facing tough challenges. During this time, the Moose card kept coming up every single time I drew cards out of the deck. Moose means Stamina. That is exactly what I needed, stamina to get through my pain and to rise above my situation. Moose medicine was incredibly helpful to me.

We spent several more nights in the car, parking wherever we could find a safe spot and washing up in public restrooms. After a couple of nights I was exhausted and decided to rent a hotel room. I didn't have the money for the room but wrote a check anyway, hoping my paycheck the next day would clear the bank before the check did. Relief was in sight. It was nearly payday and I was planning on spending the weekend at my parents' house. This would give me at least a few days to figure out my next plan of action.

Even though my parents didn't understand what I was going through, they agreed to let Shawn and I stay with them until I could figure out what I was going to do. It was a very stressful time because they didn't understand or particularly support my decision to leave

Sam. They encouraged me to try to work things out with him; after all, we had a son together. From their perspective it was just one more example of my leaving a relationship without giving it my all. I had a steady job and it appeared to them that I was the one creating the chaos in my marriage. I couldn't really blame my parents for not understanding. I just couldn't talk to them about the reality of the hellish life we had been living.

The 90-minute commute from my parent's house in Olympia to my job in Burien was through hectic morning traffic. It got old fast. I needed my space and I knew they were making sacrifices in order for Shawn and I to share their home. Not having come up with a better plan, I decided to return to the Sanctuary.

One weekend I had the place to myself. Sam and the room mates were off camping and Shawn was with my parents. An old wooden flower pot sitting on the back porch caught my eye. The thought of a drum came into my mind. I had never made a drum before, nor had I even thought about making one, but the idea of turning this old flower pot into a drum kept recurring. I grabbed the pot and cleaned it up, removing the dead plant and soil and washing it clean. I set the washed pot on the kitchen table and grabbed some paints from another project. I painted each strip of wood on the pot a different color. As I worked, I wondered just how I would transform the pot into a drum. It suddenly came to me to look up leather workers in the phone book. I found one not too far away so I drove to the shop having no idea what I would find.

Entering the store I immediately saw a piece of cow hide that might work. I talked to the clerk who explained how to soak the hide to make it pliable and how to mold it around the pot. I bought the hide and cut it into a round shape that would fold over the pot when it was soft. I soaked the leather hide and from the trimmings, cut strips that could be used as string. I worked on my little drum through the evening and couldn't wait to play it the next morning.

After breakfast I prepared a comfortable place for myself in the living room. Sitting on a pillow with my legs crossed and cuddling the drum in the middle of my lap, I started drumming with no particular agenda or rhythm. I closed my eyes and continued drumming losing myself in the beat. All of a sudden a man with unruly white hair came to me. I knew I had seen his face somewhere before but was unsure of who he was. I remembered seeing the face on posters along with the equation $E=mc^2$. Of course it was Albert Einstein! I knew who he was, but not having a particularly strong academic background or mindset I knew little, and certainly had never studied him.

I didn't drum too much longer. I was so excited about this famous guy coming to me. I could hardly wait until the next day when I could stop at the library to do research during my lunch. Maybe I would find a clue as to why this guy had come through. Several interesting things I discovered were his penchant for philosophy and how he received important information through dreams. I had recently started studying my dreams so was happy to share this connection with such a smart guy.

I was also opening myself up to messages from animals and creature beings; not only through the cards, but by paying attention to my environment. I became very aware of the crows. Whenever I went outside into the yard, the crows flew around voicing their distinctive caw sound. I got the impression they were telling me things were going to get better. I felt more peaceful and confident my life was about to change. I had no idea just how dramatic the change would be.

The same weekend I made the drum, I spotted a dead crow in a planter box outside a window. Earlier in the day, they had cawed at me so this felt distinctly like a sign, but one I didn't understand. As I sat looking past the dead crow towards the street, in my line of vision was a black cat at the very end of the drive way. A chill went through my body. The cat sat as still as a statue. I just knew the cat had something to do with the crow. Under the ceaseless stare of the cat, I began to get restless. I went into the kitchen to fix something to eat. I had been gone for at least 20 minutes when I came back into the room and again looked out the window. The black cat was still sitting in the same place, which struck me as very strange. But what was even stranger, the dead crow was no longer in the flower box. Again I got shivers and thought this was more than just a random occurrence. I was so excited knowing I was experiencing a supernatural moment; I started jumping up and down. I looked back into the yard and the black cat was gone. Later that afternoon, I opened the front door and wasn't surprised to see the dead crow lying in front of the door. If I had not looked down, I am sure I would have stepped on it. I was even more surprised when I looked up and spied the black cat sitting exactly where he had been earlier. I walked towards him and he ran away.

My ex-husband Matt along with our son, Jesse, relocated to Oregon, a five-hour drive from where I lived. It was a long distance to travel to pick him up for our scheduled visits. My parents helped out by meeting Matt half-way and bringing Jesse back to their house so I could see him. One evening when I arrived with Shawn, Jesse was particularly excited to see me. He had something for me. As he handed the little box to me, my mom interjected, "Lacey, you will not believe how your son acted today! Before you open that, let me tell you what happened." I held the box in my hand as I listened to mom tell her story.

After meeting Matt and Jesse at a truck stop, they decided to eat breakfast before driving back home. While they paid for breakfast, Jesse was interested in trinkets displayed in a glass case. He pointed to one piece and insisted he wanted to get it for me. When my mom told him I didn't need it, he proceeded to throw the biggest fit ever. This was completely out of character for him. Typically he was a good kid and well behaved in public. My parents were so surprised by his reaction, they decided to buy the necklace for him. On the drive to the house, all he could talk about was the necklace and how much I was going to love it.

I opened the gift box and squealed in delight. I couldn't believe my eyes. I started jumping up and down and hugging Jesse. The necklace was shaped like an arrowhead with insets of turquoise. I excitedly explained to my mom what Spirit Wolf had told me about my guide, Wind Maker, placing the necklace around my neck. Now spirit was offering me confirmation making the words materialize in my real life. It helped put my doubts about the credibility of the spirit world to rest.

Truly it was a confirmation the physical world mirrors the spirit world beyond our five senses. Is it not written and do we not pray "Thy will be done on Earth as it is in Heaven"? Ultimately all things are willed and spoken into being. There have been many times my mother has looked askance at me, but to date this was certainly one of the strangest looks she had ever given me.

Every morning I left early for work so I could spend time driving around looking for an apartment. I desperately wanted to live by the water even though I didn't have the faintest idea how this could come to be. I was in debt and absolutely didn't have any credit to call my own. One morning I spotted an apartment building with a "for rent" sign. I parked the car and peeked in the windows. It looked very inviting. From one corner of the living room window there was a view of Puget Sound. Breathing deeply, I could smell the fresh salty air.

I made an appointment to meet the owner the following morning. I was so excited! I didn't know how I was going to manage it, but nevertheless felt optimistic. The owner was not impressed with my work history and the fact I had been at my job for only a few months. My credit history didn't help matters either. My chances looked pretty grim. Although he said he would think about it and let me know, I didn't hear from him. I was so anxious to know, I called him as soon as I got off work that day. The answer was "no". He figured my income was not sufficient to pay the rent based on estimates of my total expenses. I was heartbroken. I knew we needed to get our own place soon.

My life was in flux. Sometimes both Shawn and I stayed with my parents; sometimes I left him with them while I slept at the Sanctuary. Occasionally I took Shawn to the Sanctuary with me so he could see his dad. I tolerated being around the dysfunction of the Sanctuary while I slowly sorted through our things. For the most part, things seemed to be relatively peaceful so I quietly continued to move my things out, being careful not to make waves.

Since my initiation with Spirit Wolf, I was more keenly aware of my intuition and spiritual gifts. One day as I drove down the driveway to the Sanctuary, a fleeting and seemingly random thought crossed my mind of a dead body in a pickup truck next door. I didn't give it another thought, until one of the roommates told me the next day a body had been found in the pickup truck. It was pretty mind blowing to say the least; affirming of my growing psychic gifts but also, startling. After all, it was someone's dead body. It was certainly not your everyday occurrence.

The Sanctuary continued to be "party central" for a number of people. Interestingly, there was a woman dating one of Sam's cousins who would not step foot in the house, backyard, or the Sanctuary. Her boyfriend often came by to listen to the music. If she was with him, she sat in the car or sometimes on the front lawn doing sketches. One day I asked her about it and she explained she felt something really dark in the house.

She described it as being bad energy and she didn't feel comfortable around it. I had similar feelings but hadn't quite acknowledged or articulated them. I didn't really understand how different energies can have various influences on us. I was just waking up to the fact the energy around the house and the Sanctuary where the band and their groupies hung out, was not good for me. Having this woman, who obviously was not part of the group, tell me her perception of the energy as being bad, convinced me even more that I needed to get away from this environment as soon as possible.

Before I left the sanctuary for good, the quiet voice of uneasiness escalated into a scream within me. Sam was obsessed with watching movies and videos depicting actual deaths. That was all he wanted to do and it made me sick. Some of the roommates watched the videos with him, but even they were sickened and more often than not, went into their rooms leaving Sam alone with his videos. The energy was growing darker.

I have learned through the years it is important to surround ourselves with manifestations of high vibrating and positive energy in whatever form we imagine. Examples include white light, God, the divine creator, the universe, angels, and spirit guides. When we accept or seek out people, places, and situations vibrating at very low levels where the focus is escape, drugs, violence or death, we encourage negativity in ourselves. Even music with discordant vibrations and negative or violent lyrics lower our energy and turn our minds toward dark and negative places.

When we live in lower energy, we place responsibility and power outside of ourselves, blaming others for disharmony or suspecting them of doing us wrong. We reinforce the belief that it's always someone else's fault for what's happening in our lives. There is a greater tendency to want to escape and numb ourselves with addictions to drugs, alcohol, food, sex or other obsessions.

When we surround ourselves with higher energy and seek out people, places, and situations that are loving and positive, we tend to be more conscious, especially of potentially addictive behavior. It's easier to cultivate attitudes of non-judgment and gratitude and give thanks, even when facing challenges.

On my way to work every morning I continued to drive around neighborhoods near Puget Sound. I was convinced I was going to manifest my perfect place to live near the water. My daily rounds included driving by the apartment where the owner had turned me down. It remained empty. After a couple weeks, I called the landlord and begged him to let me rent the apartment. I even told him it was mine and would remain empty until he agreed to let me have it! Again he told me "no." Disappointed but not ready to give up, I continued to drive by the apartment every morning. I pictured Shawn and me living there and playing in the baseball field next door. I drove down into the marina parking lot and visualized the two of us walking the beach. I just knew this was the area where we would live.

One morning as I drove by the empty apartment, I noticed the landlord's car in the parking lot. I stopped and got out of my car. Seeing me he shook his head "no" waving me away with his hand. I followed him through the parking lot and begged him to please rent the apartment to me. I could tell he was very frustrated with me. I told him it was my payday and if he let me rent the place, I would give him my entire check. I explained my plan to pay extra to make up the deposit and of my plans to work more hours to increase my income. I tried to persuade him by reminding him, he had wasted an entire month and threw away a month's rent by letting it remain empty. He could put a stop to it by renting me the apartment now. He didn't relent, and continued shaking his head.

I said everything I could think of to convince him, but to no avail. I thanked him and wished him a good day as I fought back my tears. Getting into my car, I saw my check book hanging half-way out of my purse. I grabbed it and found a pen. I walked over as he approached his car and waved my checkbook in the air saying, "I am writing you a check for the rent. I get paid today. Please rent me this apartment. You will not be disappointed." Without saying a word, he opened his car door and pulled out his briefcase which he placed on the hood. He mumbled unintelligibly. I held my breath wondering what would happen next. He handed a rental agreement to me. He didn't say much, but I heard him mumble something about needing a vacation.

That very morning I drove off with the keys to the apartment. I was so excited and then it hit me. How in the world was I going to pay for this apartment? I had just written a check for rent I couldn't afford. All the money I was getting paid that day had already been spent. I owed money to Shawn's daycare and several other bills for necessities were outstanding. At the daycare that afternoon, I explained I had just rented a place and I couldn't afford to pay them on time. Thankfully, my record with them was a good one and they were willing to give me a break and let it slide for a couple of weeks.

That evening, I took Shawn to my parents' house to stay for a few days so I could spend time moving our stuff to the apartment. I still didn't know how I was going to pay the rent, but I also knew it would work out. It had to! My friend the wandering gypsy said she could help out by moving in and sharing the rent for a few months. She also needed time to figure out her next move. Having a roommate really wasn't what I planned or wanted, but I was desperate.

On the day she moved in, I arrived home from work to a shocking pile of boxes trailing from one room to another throughout the apartment. She had emptied her storage unit into my living room! There was a narrow open path to the bedroom, the kitchen, and a very small space where the couch sat. The boxes literally reached the ceiling. I flipped out. I didn't realize all the stuff in her storage unit was part of the package. With all the patience I could muster, we discussed it and I agreed they could stay as long as she sorted through the boxes and got rid of some each day. As it turned out, she was hardly there. I decided it was a small price to pay having a pile of boxes as a roommate.

Thankfully it didn't last long. After just several months, the gypsy and her tower of boxes moved out. I was very grateful to her for helping me out with rent. Her arrival was divinely timed. If she had not shown up needing a place to live, I really don't know if I could have made the rent, as I had so confidently promised the landlord I would do. I had prayed for multiple things to manifest in my life and she showed up as one of them.

One day after work I drove to Sam's to get the last of our belongings. Sam didn't want me to leave him or the Sanctuary. I told him I needed a change. Things between us were only getting worse. His priorities were music and drugs, and he did not share my desire for a more normal family life. I knew I had to be careful about what I said to make the transition an easy one. He hugged me tight and momentarily I felt my resolve weaken. But in that moment I could feel his rage, and what felt like a smoldering volcano, a sense of energy trapped and building up inside him. I didn't want to be around when it finally blew. Being around him, I felt my inner power and energy being sucked from my body. Driving away there was a distinct feeling of being lost, but nevertheless, I knew there was no going back.

To earn some additional money, I took on a few cleaning jobs and agreed to help Nancy, an upstairs neighbor. She worked and studied evenings and I cooked dinner for her daughters while she was away. Nancy proved to be a true angel in disguise. We became fast friends. She was finishing up her training as a massage therapist during the day and in the evening she studied a modality called Feldenkrais to complement her work in massage. She was, and is, an incredible inspiration to me because she was a single mom with goals and doing everything she could to reach them. After working all day, I came home to cook meals for Nancy's two girls and for Shawn and me. There were many times I couldn't afford to buy food and Nancy helped out with groceries and other miscellaneous supplies like laundry soap, toilet paper, and etc.

One weekend Shawn was with my parents and Nancy asked if I'd like to go to a church service with her. Nancy's mom was going too and she thought it would be a great idea for me to go instead of staying home alone on a Saturday night. We sat in the pew and listened to a sermon with a very familiar theme with a simple message, "Fear God." I could feel my old resistance resurfacing and felt very uncomfortable. I never resonated with this message and once again was feeling angry with the idea that we should be god-fearing people. This goes against everything I believe God to be. I can't imagine a god who wants us to fear the idea of him. After what I had experienced with Sam, I knew what it was like to fear someone! If God was a God of wrath and anger, then I wanted to run as far away as I could and go my own way. Something inside me affirmed that God is love.

Following the service people mingled and talked. A woman approached me and asked how I liked the sermon. I politely said it was okay. She nodded and walked away. I sat back down and the minister came and sat beside me. He too asked how I liked the sermon. I told him quite bluntly I didn't like the references to fearing God and my God wasn't to be feared. He sat and listened. I was feeling pretty angry and frustrated with what had been happening in my personal life, so I didn't stop there. I explained I was exploring joining a coven and how these beliefs about fearing God probably incited people to persecute others and burn witches like me. He sat silent for a minute then politely told me to have a good evening and he walked away. I am sure the poor man felt all too acutely my wrath; I can't really blame him for ending our conversation. For the rest of the evening, he avoided me. I was really glad when it was time we could leave.

Sam and I never agreed on how to raise our son. Sam loved Shawn but I thought he was overly strict with him. Generally I was very uncomfortable with many things Sam did or said. Many times Shawn acted like a typical child – wanting things or trying to get attention – and Sam talked to him in a big strong deep and scary voice that even frightened me. He sent Shawn to his room expecting him to clean it up as was appropriate for a 10 year-old, but Shawn wasn't even half that age. Sam expected a lot more from Shawn than a child so young could deliver. There were a few times when he disciplined Shawn and Sam wouldn't let me listen to what he was telling him. I always got a sick feeling in my stomach when this took place, and time and time again I made sure to interrupt the discussion. Sam had a way of controlling people through intimidation. It seemed particularly dangerous as he realized he was losing his hold over me and certainly was not in control of himself or his own behavior. I didn't like the idea of him turning his attention to Shawn and working out his unhealthy need to control on our small child.

Sam historically was passive-aggressive and at times seemed like a time bomb about ready to go off. I know I wasn't the easiest person to get along with, especially as I continued to grow more confident, speaking up for myself and Shawn, and standing up for what I thought was right. I didn't' really care if his friends, or the band, or others at the Sanctuary liked me or not. Sam smoked pot in front of Shawn and I was dead set against anyone doing drugs around him. In fact when we lived together, I continually told Sam I wanted him to quit or at least cut back on his drug use which I believed contributed to his erratic and unpredictable behavior and quickly changing moods. I remember arguments when Sam would be zoned out in an almost Zen sort of way, seeming to handle our arguments with utmost control. Then unexpectedly a small thing would elicit an emotional outburst.

This inconsistency and emotional volatility made me crazy! He never seemed to live by a set of discernible rules or honor typical social mores or boundaries. If I or Shawn went against him or said or did something he didn't agree with, there was always the threat, and very real possibility, of retribution.

I quit communicating with Sam at one point because of this and avoided as often as possible, any opportunity for Shawn to be around him. I just wanted to get on with our lives; but at the same time realized Shawn was his son and I wanted to be fair. There was still a part of me that didn't want to admit something was terribly wrong with Sam and that I needed to keep Shawn and myself away from him. I was still smoking pot a few times a week to mask the pain and the stress I was going through. This was a poor coping mechanism as being zoned out on pot caused me to miss or overlook many warning signs and certainly interfered with my ability to tune into my intuition.

Smoking marijuana tends to have a numbing effect especially if used on a regular basis. It is important to recognize whether you are smoking, drinking or eating to avoid or deny a feeling of something missing within you or your life. I think marijuana use is beneficial for some people for pain management and a viable alternative to prescription drugs, some of which I believe are more dangerous than pot. Although I believe it is best for our general well being to eat in an organic way, and to abstain from drugs and alcohol, I also recognize the role these items play in our society and especially in celebrations, and believe it is possible to enjoy them in moderation.

A few months after I moved out of the Sanctuary for good, Sam started living with the ex-girlfriend of one of the roommates. (Not surprisingly, she was the musician I had accused him of sleeping with the morning he choked me). I decided it would be okay to have Shawn spend an occasional weekend with him as long as he was with this woman. She had a son Shawn's age and I felt as a mother, she had it reasonably together.

Shawn and her son had often played together when we lived in the house with Sam. It gave me a little comfort to know a motherly figure would be around while Shawn was visiting.

One weekend I had plans to go camping as part of a women's retreat honoring the Goddess in ourselves. I was really looking forward to a weekend of dancing, doing crafts, hiking, and receiving healing for body, mind and spirit. I dropped Shawn off at Sam's girlfriend's place and noticed I didn't feel quite right. My heart hurt as I was leaving. I dismissed the feeling as part of the emotional release I was experiencing recently as a result of doing some very deep healing work. I was learning to forgive myself for the guilt and shame I still felt so acutely over losing custody of Jesse and for the many mistakes I blamed myself for in allowing it to happen. I was coming to terms with the fact that if I had not been with Sam during my custody battle, I probably would have won; and would have Jesse with me. It was the first time I really allowed myself to feel my emotions about this situation. Needless to say, I would burst into tears in the most inopportune times. So it wasn't surprising to me I was all teary-eyed and sad when dropping Shawn off that day.

I went to the women's retreat and continued to feel sick. I tried to have fun and get into the crafts and the dancing, but instead, developed a terrible migraine headache. Someone offered to massage me to release some of the pressure I was feeling. She had the kindest and most loving energy and I felt safe and comforted. Nevertheless, half-way through the session, I jumped off the table, and went outside to throw up. I continued to feel really awful. I decided at that moment I needed to leave. I packed up my tent and headed home. As I was driving, rain started pouring down. While still driving on the highway, my windshield wipers quit working. I kept asking myself "God what am I not seeing?"

I got to my apartment and called Sam's girlfriend's house to tell him I was coming to get Shawn early. The person who answered the phone informed me they were not there. This angered me because I had told Sam he needed to stay there if he was going to have Shawn with him. Still feeling extremely ill, I wanted more than ever to get Shawn. The rain had let up, but I knew it might not be for long. I took my chances anyway in hopes of finding Shawn and Sam. I stopped at his girlfriend's house, but they still were not there. I drove over to the Sanctuary and pulled into the driveway with a sense of dread. This was the last place I wanted to be; and it was the last place I wanted to find Shawn.

There was no answer in response to my knocking on the house door so I walked around to the back and looked through a window. There was Shawn. He saw me and came running out, grabbing my leg and holding on tight. I asked him about his dad and he said Sam was sleeping.

I walked into Sam's bedroom. Someone else was in the bed with him but I didn't care. I was furious. I started yelling and the person in the bed scooted further under the covers. I told Sam I hated him for going back on his word and not keeping Shawn over at his girlfriend's house or rather, his ex-girlfriend, since she was obviously not the woman in his bed. I grabbed Shawn and started out the door but not before I came back and demanded money. I knew he had recently been paid so I figured I might as well take it while he had it.

That night while giving Shawn a bath, I noticed a mark on his thumb which looked like a burn. Instantly my mind went to a memory of a story Sam had shared with me about a childhood experience. I wondered, "Could Sam have burned Shawn in the same way he had been tortured and burned in his troubled youth?" (My research and reading has revealed it is very possible for a person to replicate injuries inflicted upon them.) I asked Shawn what had happened and he squirmed like he didn't want to talk about it. After much prodding, Shawn finally reported Sam's dog did it. Later a nurse confirmed it did in fact look very much like a burn mark.

The next time Sam called, I asked him what happened to Shawn's thumb and he told me the dog had bitten him. It is possible that considering the chaos and number of people hanging around the Sanctuary, Sam might genuinely not have known what happened to Shawn. Knowing I would be upset, he might have made up the story about the dog and convinced Shawn to go along with it. The explanation didn't sit right with me and from that time forward, I made excuses when Sam called asking to see Shawn. Today more than ever I am convinced the premonitions of danger at the Sanctuary had to do with my son.

Years later when I read reports of the crime scene analysis involving the kidnapping that landed Sam in jail, I learned the girl had a burn mark on her right thumb. It sent shivers up my spine.

Living on my own I was finally turning my life around. I was learning as much as I could about past life regression by taking a certification in hypnotherapy. I had become a Reiki Master and was participating in a sweat lodge once a month. I was inviting people over to my apartment to walk them through guided meditation, do energy work on them or take them into a past life. I was studying the Futhark runes every week at a metaphysical store. I was also recording my dreams and writing a lot.

I heard about a technique called Holographic Reprogramming. The price was reasonable - only $25 a session – so I decided I would try it out. As I was laying face down on a massage table, the practitioner started working on me. I drifted in and out of consciousness. I wondered how this gal working on me could be touching all the areas she was touching as quickly as she seemed to be touching them. She would have to be moving around the table at a very quick pace in order to be doing what I was feeling. All of a sudden I got a vision of what was happening. I found myself outside of my body observing other worldly beings surrounding me as I lay on the table. They were poking me with their fingers and letting them rest in different areas for a few seconds before they moved on to another area. My body jerked and buzzed. I could feel the energy racing through my body. As the session came to an end, I awoke with a greater sense of clarity. Afterwards I told the practitioner I had seen several beings around the table during the session. She smiled and said she wasn't surprised; other clients had reported having similar experiences.

I left that evening full of energy and excitement, while at the same time, feeling extremely relaxed and content. As I drove home I was listening to the radio and not really thinking about anything, when all of a sudden something kicked the back of my seat. The movement was hard enough to make me physically jerk. Startled, I looked in the rear view mirror and for split second I saw what I would describe as an extraterrestrial being. I turned my head towards the back seat and waved my arm back and forth behind me, trying to feel something; but nothing and no one was there. My heart pounded and I felt nervous but not really scared.

I thought about the incident for a few days, wondering what exactly it was and whether or not I had imagined the whole thing. Then it happened again a few weeks later. I was in the passenger seat this time, riding with an acquaintance to a drumming circle. She was explaining what to expect at the drum gathering when I felt a hard nudge from the back of my seat. It felt as if someone in the back seat was kicking my seat. The feeling was not as hard as the first time, but still jolted me. I looked in the back seat to see if maybe something had fallen against my seat, but just like the first time, nothing was there. I looked at the driver and she was still talking, unaware of anything unusual, or that I was distracted and looking around. Since I didn't know this woman very well, I kept it to myself. I couldn't help but think about it throughout the evening and on the way back home.

It would be several years before I was given a name for my new, other worldly visitor, maybe because I didn't bother to ask his name until several years later.

When guides and angels show up and you want to know who it is, or what to call the energy you are feeling, it is as simple as asking. Even if the name you hear is a common name or possibly the name of someone in your life like a friend or sister, don't think you are making it up. Our guides and angels are messengers from God as long as we are vibrating in the white light. They are not as attached to having a name, as much as we are to having a name to call them. There are also archangels who can be called upon by name with special gifts to offer. Angel means messenger of God.

Once a week, I perused the shelves of the second-hand book store. I have always been an avid reader and at the time was studying anything I could get my hands on, in the areas of metaphysics, self help, and psychology. I reached to pull a book off the shelf when a small paperback, old and yellowed, fell to the floor. There staring up at me was the face of a Native American man. The book was called "Lame Deer Seeker of Visions." Some of the pages were torn and it smelled musty and damp; but something about the book appealed to me. I forgot about the other book, and instantly knew the old paperback in my hand was the book I came to get that day.

I started reading it right away and found I couldn't walk away from it. His story struck a chord within me. I felt the pain, strength, and courage of this man. He felt so familiar, like I knew him. Even though I finished reading the book in record time, I carried it with me for months.

In the book, he described how he had taken rocks, with his bare hands, out of the middle of an ant pile for strength and power. I felt moved to do the same thing.

Near my parent's home, there was a couple of big ant hills that had been there since I was a child. I knew it would be more powerful if I got the rocks from a place I played as a child, so the next time I visited my parents, I walked down into the field towards the creek to find the ant hills.

There were lots of red ants crawling quickly from place to place. I stood staring at the pile wondering just how, like Lame Deer, I was going to dig into the pile with my bare hands. I started digging. The ants however didn't appear to share my vision. Quickly they crawled up my arms and I started waving my arms in the air to shake them off. I figured it wasn't the best thing to do to the poor ants since after all, I was invading their home. I knelt on the ground and watched as the ants busily went about mending the hole I had made. I wasn't quite sure how I was going to do this without getting angry ants crawling up and down my arm. Then I remembered I was supposed to pray and ask permission of the ants to take the precious rocks out of their home.

I took a deep breath and prayed for permission to enter their sacred hill. Prayer seemed to have the same effect on the ants, as a beekeeper's smoke does on bees, because they immediately became calmer and I started digging again. This time the ants avoided my arm as I picked little pebbles out of the middle of the hill. I placed them in a sea shell I brought as a container. After collecting over 50 small stones, I took the pebbles home and placed the sea shell and its precious contents on my altar.

Eleven months after I moved out of the Sanctuary, with no warning, the FBI showed up at my door to ask me about Sam. The word about him being a suspect in a kidnapping case spread quickly and my phone started ringing. My parents too were barraged with calls from people trying to get a hold of me. Thankfully my parents protected my privacy and didn't give my number out, but instead, passed messages and caller phone numbers on to me.

People I hadn't seen or talked to in years, now wanted to talk with me. It was natural for them to be curious. I had been Sam's girlfriend on and off for five years and was the mother of his son. Everyone wanted to know what I was thinking and where I stood. The story of 9-year old little girl missing from her home, was plastered all over the news. Sam appeared to be the number one suspect and reportedly the last one to be seen with the little girl.

The authorities eventually found Sam at Rainbow Valley just as I had suggested when they questioned me. They took him in for questioning and he agreed to a lie detector test. (He told me later he passed.) They apparently didn't have sufficient evidence, because he was released. The authorities initiated a stakeout to keep track of his every move. The police had no other leads.

The thought of what the parents of the little girl were going through played on my mind and heart. I couldn't imagine how I would feel if one of my boys was missing. I felt I had to do something to help. I figured if Sam was involved or knew something, maybe he would confide in me. I thought about how remorseful he felt after he strangled me that time. Maybe he just needed someone to turn to for support. I decided to go down alone to visit Sam to see if I could get any information that might help everyone involved, especially the little girl.

As I drove into the trailer park, I noticed a man sitting in a parked car across from the trailer where Sam was staying. He watched me as I got out of my car and walked to the trailer and knocked. Sam answered the door, invited me in, and told me about the hideous allegations being brought against him. He was angry. The authorities had taken his clothes and leather coat. He had to borrow clothes from a friend. I felt very uncomfortable in this place and suggested we go to a park near the water where we used to go together. As we walked to my car, Sam walked over to the agent in the parked car. I didn't know what he was doing, and headed to my car and waited for him. When Sam got into the car, he explained he was just saving some chaos by telling the agent where we were headed. If he hadn't, chances are the authorities would have pulled me over and harassed me because he was in my car. They were keeping a close eye on him.

The agent followed us and it wasn't long before I realized there were several other official looking cars all in succession behind us. I felt like I had landed in the middle of some big mobster take down. I decided I would pull through a McDonald's drive-through to grab a bite to eat. Sam was stressed because I was not following the route he had told the agent we were going to take. Three cars pulled into the lot behind us and Sam continued complaining that it wasn't a good idea. I retorted I was hungry and it was highly unlikely we would escape or lose them while sitting in the McDonald's drive-through. I was right; following our brief detour, we led the entourage to the park where each of the three cars parked in different areas of the lot. I agreed with Sam, we better tell them we were taking a walk and would be back in a short while.

As we walked down the path towards the Narrows Bridge, I questioned him as thoroughly as I could. Since I had been taking hypnotherapy training, I was convinced I could get him to relax. There was even an outside chance he would fall into a light hypnotic state and I might be able to find out all he knew about the little girl's disappearance. We found a huge boulder, warmed by the sun, and perfect to sit on. I told him maybe he did have information that might help with the investigation; and suggested that if he let me hypnotize him, we might find a vital clue to help the investigation and prove his innocence. I reassured him there was nothing to fear, but he was adamant this wasn't going to happen. He didn't want to talk about what was going on. Instead he repeatedly changed the subject asking me questions about Shawn and me. I was frustrated that he kept steering the conversation back to us.

After more than an hour, he suggested we start back to the car saying the authorities would have the dogs after us. We decided to take an alternate route back to the park, one that took us off the trail, through blackberry bushes and down the railroad tracks. Sam was right. The officials had brought in search dogs and were apparently ready to look for us. As we returned to my car, the dogs and their handlers followed. The agent I had first noticed at the trailer park walked over to my car and suggested we take the most direct path back to the trailer park. The look on his face left no doubt; if I was smart I would follow his recommendation.

I was disappointed. I still had no real idea about what was going on with him. He had not divulged anything meaningful. Again, the thought crossed my mind, "maybe there isn't anything to divulge." I dropped him off and headed home. It wasn't long before an agent showed up at my door and asked me about our meeting and whether or not Sam had shared anything of substance with me. I told the truth. He hadn't told me anything.

I cooperated with the detectives by answering their questions about Sam and the case. I willingly shared some of my concerns about strange behavior I had observed in Sam prior to the July incident. I wanted to cooperate as much as possible because I didn't want them to question Shawn. Several times they had suggested talking with Shawn and I said "no". At one point I adamantly stated they could subpoena me but if they tried to talk with Shawn, we would surely disappear and would not cooperate, even if it meant I had to go to jail. Shawn had already gone through so much with the dysfunctional life we had been living, I wasn't going to let it get worse by allowing the authorities to badger him with all sorts of questions. Our life was in order and everything was finally feeling normal. I wanted to shield myself from further information about the case and ended up secluding myself even more.

Life continued, but it was certainly different. I was frustrated with all the attention focused on my past involvement with Sam. Friends and family continued calling, ostensibly because they were concerned. I couldn't help thinking they were fishing for more information than what the media was providing. I didn't have a television so was not really aware of the continuing coverage. I wasn't interested in what anyone had to say about any of it. When well-meaning family and friends would start to fill me in on the latest news, I would interrupt them and tell them I didn't want to hear any of it. I didn't want to know anything about what was going on. The only thing I was concerned about was the safety of the little girl. I wanted to know when she was found.

A couple of nights before I got news her body had been found, I dreamed of being in a yard that was run down and unkempt. I was standing in the driveway which had become somewhat overgrown with weeds. Even though I didn't see a rug in my dream, I was yelling at Sam about a rug. I was furious and kept demanding more information from him. He didn't say anything in the dream. He stood looking at me with a bewildered look on his face. I woke up shaking, feeling all the anger I had felt in my dream. I got up and couldn't quite shake this uneasy feeling. I felt very emotional as well as helpless but I kept pushing through my day hoping it would pass.

I was very grateful I was working for an understanding boss who knew what I was going through. She was very supportive of Shawn and me. One day when a reporter showed up at the store, in hopes of talking with me, my boss kindly told the man I preferred to not be involved. Luckily for me he never tried contacting me again. All I wanted to do was to be in seclusion with Shawn, away from anyone who even mentioned the horrific events taking place.

My body turned cold when I heard the little girl was found dead in a rug. I was in shock and immediately remembered the dream. During this time I was having fierce migraines that wouldn't quit. I often left work early, grabbed Shawn from daycare and rushed home or to the water to get out into the fresh air. I was very overwhelmed by all that was going on. I felt sick for the parents of this child and I felt sick that somehow I was involved by association.

About a month after the little girl's body was discovered, there was a knock on the door. I ran to open it and my heart skipped a beat. It was Sam. For a split second I saw a little girl standing beside him smiling up at me. I started to cry. I was so confused and didn't know what to say. I certainly didn't share this vision with Sam as he took me into his arms thinking that my crying was because of him. I couldn't believe what I had just seen. Was it my imagination? My mind raced as Sam stood in the doorway telling me he had borrowed this cool trench coat (the police had taken his) and some friends had dropped him off at the bus station in Tacoma so he could take a bus all the way up here to see Shawn and me. He said he had walked several miles from the bus station just to see us. I wondered how he got my address and remembered one of our mutual friends had been here several months earlier to drop off the rest of my things.

Shawn ran out of his room very excited about seeing his dad. He asked Sam to come into his room and play. I took a couple deep breaths trying to clear my mind of the vision I had just seen. I was also trying to figure out what I was going to do. In response to my asking him what he was doing here, he answered he was hoping to stay with us. Shawn started jumping up and down at the possibility; but my heart sank. It sank even further when Shawn told his dad he could sleep in his room. I was heart-broken. I didn't know how I was going to handle this, but I knew every nerve in my body was shaking with sheer tension and stress.

I told Sam he needed to leave and that he couldn't stay with us. I explained he had too many things he needed to deal with right now and I didn't want to be involved. Sam looked very disappointed and tears rolled down his face. I know he was hoping I would support him like I had done so many times before. I am an eternal optimist and always made light of every negative situation that had come up in our past relationship. I am a trooper and usually willing to go all the way in supporting those I loved.

However this day, I couldn't do that. I asked him to leave. Sam cried and Shawn sobbed. He didn't want his dad to leave. Sam looked at me with pleading eyes. I had never seen this look before; not in the five turbulent years we had been together. I was sick inside. It was as if I was kicking a lost puppy out into the cold.

He kept hesitating, stopping, and turning around like I was going to change my mind any minute. I shut the door and leaned against it with tears falling down my face and Shawn clinging to my leg crying.

A few minutes later, Shawn and I went upstairs to Nancy's apartment. I didn't know what to do, or if I had done the right thing. What I did know was I needed to talk to someone. Sam walked by her window and knocked on the door. When I opened it, he reminded me I had told him about some runes I had made, and said he could have them. As if it hadn't been hard enough, by this time, I just wanted it to be over. I wasn't very nice to him as I lead him downstairs to get the runes. It took every bit of strength I could muster to stay firm in my resolve to have him leave and not come back. My body would not let me do otherwise, even though I could sense he wanted nothing more than for me to take him back and give him refuge.

The following day, I filed a restraining order against him. I wanted to ensure we were left alone. I didn't want to be bothered by him or the authorities anymore. When I went to the courthouse for the restraining order I slipped and fell. It was as if someone had come up behind and pushed me. When I looked around, there was no one there.

Sam was also there with his girlfriend and continued glaring at me. I explained to the judge I wanted to keep a distance between us because of the ongoing investigation. The judge declined my request. Nancy and I stood there in shock. We couldn't believe it had been denied. As Nancy and I walked to the elevator, Sam approached us looking very angry. His girlfriend was following behind telling him to calm down. He started yelling at us. He accused Nancy and me of child abuse and all sorts of crazy things. Nancy and I stood in disbelief. I looked around to see if anyone was coming to our aid but it was as if we were invisible. Sam's girlfriend continued to try to pull him away from us. Finally the elevator door opened. We didn't know whether we should get in or not, but Sam was letting his girlfriend pull him in another direction. He yelled a warning that we would get what was coming to us.

The denial of the restraining order was unfathomable to me. It was also unbelievable that not one single person in the courthouse came to our defense or tried to help when he was verbally assaulting us that day. The only thing I could imagine is the judge believed Sam was already under investigation and the restraining order was unnecessary and would add to the confusion.

I realized I needed as much spiritual help as I could get, if I was to remain safe and sound and protected from mental, emotional and physical harm. I looked to God and the Angels to watch over Shawn and me.

I received several more calls from Sam. I just couldn't deal with him so I let the phone machine take the calls. His messages concerned me. Sometimes he cried and begged for help. Other times he was angry because I was keeping him away from our son. At one point he threatened me and talked to me with a very evil tone in his voice. He sounded desperate and at the end of his rope. Because I cared about him, even still loved him, it was very hard to listen to these messages. However, I reminded myself we were not together, not a couple, and he was not my problem anymore.

Jesse spent the summer with me and Shawn and then returned back home with his dad in Oregon. It was always hard to see him go and I missed him. I kept very busy doing my best imitation of super woman. I was a single mom working full time and chauffeuring my son back and forth to piano lessons and karate workouts. And my creative side was no slouch either. I was into drums, faerie realms, and creating dream catchers and masks composed of mosses, leaves and sticks. I wasn't sleeping very well at night. I tossed and turned and often woke up crying and full of sweat following a nightmare that filled me with lingering fear.

One afternoon Shawn and I went with Richard, a long-time friend, into the mountains to see the meteor showers. It was late afternoon when we arrived. We poked around in some old logs and I was very tickled to find pieces of amber. At dusk, we climbed a hill and sat down to watch the sunset. It was a great place to watch for the meteors. We were making small talk, when all of a sudden, I heard a voice speak into my left ear, "Fuck you" in a really deep and scary voice. It was as if someone had come up behind me and aggressively yelled into my ear. I was visibly shaken. When I asked Richard if he had heard it, he looked at me as if he didn't have a clue as to what I was talking about. Shawn and Richard were both sitting on my right side so I knew neither of them was responsible. Besides I couldn't imagine either of them doing such a thing.

I was restless and anxious the remainder of the evening while we watched the sky. It was such a relief when we left for home and Shawn and I arrived back at our apartment. I carried Shawn into his room and tucked him in for the night. I immediately changed my clothes and crawled into bed. My night was filled with horrific nightmares of dark occult visions and screaming children. Tossing and turning, I wondered about these fierce forces and about the voice I heard on the mountain earlier that evening. I had not yet learned I could surround myself with love and light and be protected from dark energies and forces simply by asking. I was still learning I could ask for God, the Universe, or Spirit for help.

Divine timing was evident as the next morning I started doing the Master Mind Prayer with my neighbor Nancy. (Master Mind Prayer developed by Reverend Jack Boland is an 8-step prayer process which is recited by like-minded positive people intending to support their lives and the lives of others using the power of prayer.) It became a daily ritual for me and soon the darkness started lifting. Life was getting better and we were finding a way to make each day count. A month later, Sam was arrested for the kidnapping, rape and murder of the 9-year old girl.

I enjoyed my job but nevertheless was not content or completely satisfied being a regional assistant. Being a single mom, my life was filled with activity, but I didn't feel fulfilled. I loved my boss; she was the greatest so it made it easy to show up and be positive. She was a great inspiration. I witnessed her dealing with the many daily crises typical of overseeing retail stores. Day after day she put out the fires. She had a way with words and she also knew how to listen. She loved her job. She encouraged, coached, and most of all listened to me when I needed to talk. But still, I knew there must be something more for me.

I decided to volunteer for the Domestic Abuse Women's Network (DAWN). I felt moved to help other women struggling with low self esteem and living in dangerous situations. I answered calls coming in on the crisis hotline, talking to women caught up in situations I knew all too well. Many were mirrors of some of my past experiences. My goal was to inspire these women and show them they could get out of an abusive situation. I wanted them to feel they were not going through the situation alone and there were others who understood what they were going through. This work was very satisfying and healing to my soul. I even received awards and recognition for my dedication and the number of hours I spent supporting the women each month. Little did I know, this was a peek into my future.

WOLF IN SHEEP'S CLOTHING

My life experiences, including living on my own and raising my sons by myself have motivated me to translate my experiences into service to other woman who have gone through trials and tribulations similar to mine. There are so many women plagued with low self esteem that keeps them stuck in bad situations and scared to take a risk that will empower them. I know from personal experience we can open our prison doors and be freed. One way I decided to help was by volunteering at a women's domestic abuse center. I wanted to be available to women at night, when support might be especially lacking. I answered a hotline women could call anytime they were in danger, needed a listening ear, or wanted to know about tools and strategies for leaving a potentially dangerous situation. I loved this work and believed I was doing something of real worth with each call and conversation.

I was able to help other woman going through situations similar to those I had come through. It not only gave the callers comfort in knowing the person on the end of the line understood their situation, but it helped them find the strength to make changes to live safer and healthier lives. I attribute this beginning to a foundation for my later work as an on-line intuitive advisor.

I believe in order to learn something we need to start teaching it. If we wait to become masters, the world is deprived of our unique and growing personal expertise. There is an old adage that says "It is in teaching we are taught," and this certainly rings true for me. We learn so much more about ourselves by stepping out and teaching and supporting others. It is important to remember if something comes up we don't know, we need to be honest about not knowing. If we are questioned and don't have an answer, the right response is to admit it and offer to find the answer or refer to someone else who does know.

Even when going through challenging trials and tribulations, I shared my knowledge with others in an effort to empower them. I am sure some people have gotten what they needed to learn from an abusive relationship the first time around. I am not ashamed to say I was not so lucky; it has taken me many times around. I have not always been able to say that about myself. I used to beat myself up for it. It is a process. Every person's process or journey is unique and it is important not to measure yourself based on another's progress. Before I knew it my life was about to encounter more emotional abuse.

My priorities included living a healthy lifestyle and taking care of my two boys. It was a slow and long journey, but I was healing and getting past the pain of losing custody of Jesse. I was encouraged by the possibility of having him back with me when he turned twelve years old. I could hardly wait. This alone kept me going at times when I slipped into regret or guilt and uselessly wished things were different. The future would be different. Every year that passed, I was one year closer to having him live with me once again. In the meantime Shawn and I were happy, spending our evenings in the park, taking piano lessons or being home together. Fridays were our special night to go out for Mexican food. It was something we both looked forward to doing each week.

I met Don on a Friday night in the Laundromat. After enjoying our Mexican dinner, Shawn usually hung out with the neighbor girls while I did laundry. I liked doing this task on Friday nights. The Laundromat was quiet and I had time to think. It was my version of alone time.

The night I met Don, I was reading a book, but very aware of this man looking at me as he folded his clothes. He cleared his throat and asked what I was reading. "It is a book on Reiki, a form of hands-on healing" I answered looking back down at my book. I tried not to notice this good-looking Hispanic man with buckets of charisma standing there watching me. Honestly, considering all I was going through, he looked like the knight in shining armor many of us dream will rescue us from peril. He came off as very intelligent and charming. He had ironed seams down his jeans and wore a sports jacket. Every hair was in place. His speech was elegant and his voice was soft. This one knew how to make a lady feel good.

We hit it off right away. He asked for my number and called a week later to ask me out. I suppose it was very telling that he was an hour late for our date. This should have clued me into his true nature. His excuse was he was working and couldn't get to a phone to call me. I forgave him. Besides, working sounded like a good excuse and I am a very forgiving person. He wined and dined me by taking me to the most expensive restaurant in town. He made me feel like a queen. I fell head-over-heels for him.

I was extremely lonely and frustrated by having to raise my youngest son by myself. I had been looking into the Big Brother organization to get some mentoring for Shawn, and was told they had a waiting list of 6 months. I wanted Shawn to have a positive male role model in his life. Don worked with kids as an intervention specialist in a local school and I thought I had found the role model I wanted for Shawn. What I later came to realize was how very controlling Don behaved. In truth, he didn't have his own life under control so he wanted to control everything and everyone else around him.

He was still seeing a woman he met when he was a minister of a church. This affair eventually led to the dissolution of his marriage. She was in the picture for a brief time in the beginning of our relationship but at the time, I was unaware of their history. Much later one of his daughters shared the details with me but I was already hooked. I was so desperate for a partner, and someone to share in my life, I ignored the warning signs. Red flags continued to appear, but I was willing to ignore them.

Don invited me to one of his speaking engagements on an Apache reservation in Arizona. I flew down a few days after him and was very disappointed upon arrival, when he introduced me as just a friend of the family. The group he was speaking to had met his wife several years before. He believed it wouldn't look good for him if they realized he was divorced. He decided it would be a good idea if no one knew we were more than friends. I was confused. Don and I were staying with his parents and they too, along with the pastor of the church, were complicit with the lie. I was hurt but tried to not let it eat at me. What could I do? I imagined what it would be like to tell my own lie – to say we were already married and create quite a scene. But in the end I accepted the role of "family friend", a convincing story since I arrived at the church with Don's parents making it appear I was with them and not with Don.

Despite my disappointment, there were rewards of another kind in this experience. The time on the reservation turned out to be an incredible two days of magic. The people were incredibly nice to me and it was a positive emotional and spiritual experience. I took pictures of Don speaking in the church built of straw where everyone stood as they listened. I watched as waves of people, responding to the message of the Holy Spirit, fell to the ground overcome by the experience. I truly felt the presence of God that day and was also pleasantly surprised I didn't hear anything about fearing God. (I cringed once when Don talked about submitting.) I walked away from the presentation feeling full of the Holy Spirit and was grateful for the experience.

About a month later, I was looking at one of the pictures I had taken and noticed a very obscure white outline of Jesus on the cross. The image was clearly visible in the background within a window frame. I compared the picture with the negative and saw the image clearly there as well. Jesus was on the cross and he was smiling. There was light shining from every direction from his heart. I was in awe. I took it as a sign Jesus was here for me.

From that day forward I have talked to Jesus every day and he likes it that I haven't put him on a pedestal like so many others do. He wishes we would allow him to walk next to us as a friend, so that is what I do. Anytime I want to get down with Jesus I listen to the song "Jesus is just alright with me" by the Doobie Brothers and dance and praise along with Jesus.

My relationship with Don wasn't quite so fulfilling or inspiring. His words were often demeaning towards me and his actions confirmed he considered me less than desirable. He even went so far as to insinuate I was "damaged goods" and would never get anywhere without him. His words and attitudes resonated with my own beliefs and fears. In effect, I was in "recovery" and still very much blaming myself for what I saw as a lack of gumption. I was the first and the best at beating myself up for not having the common sense and means to leave Sam before I did. I was ashamed about turning a blind eye to that situation and not acting sooner. These feelings fueled my passion and determination to inspire and empower other women in similar circumstances. I wanted to do so much more than just answer the crisis line as a volunteer, but wasn't sure exactly what that would look like.

Don often reminded me his previous experience as the minister of one of the largest churches in Arizona, would be useful to me. He could help me in assisting others. However, later I was able to see that his helping me included a large dose of sabotage as well. As I would demonstrate a little success here or there, he would subtly, but powerfully push me off my pedestal. I believe it was a form of jealousy and envy of my success. He reminded me on a regular basis I was damaged goods because of my involvement with Sam and that no one else would want me. Don had a short fuse, and almost anything, and sometimes it seemed everything, set him off. Thankfully, Jesus had my back; and I was, for the most part, able to maintain a positive outlook. Consistent with my relationship pattern, I was determined to stay and make this one work. Don and I had great things to do together, or so I believed.

There was another influential man in my life – my dad. He was diagnosed with prostate cancer and I was eager to find a natural remedy to help facilitate a healing for him. There was at least anecdotal evidence Apache Tears had been effective in treating this diagnosis. I brought a handful of these stones to my dad and instructed him to carry them in his pocket. I also gave him a book of natural remedies that might complement his on-going treatments. I was convinced this would help him. I don't know if he followed any of my advice or whether or not he carried the stones. He just laughs whenever I ask him about it. More than anything, I am convinced his positive outlook and light-hearted sense of humor throughout this ordeal contributed to his ultimate healing.

In a sense, I received a healing along with him as I learned to appreciate my dad more than I had ever thought I could. I realized no matter what I had gone through, he had always been there for me, offering his advice. I remember too, that sometimes I didn't want to hear it! He supported me even when he didn't agree with my actions. He has always been there for me and my sister and for my mom. For as long as I can remember, Valentine's Day was special for dad. He always shows his appreciation for us with gifts of flowers, chocolates, coffee gift cards, gift certificates to restaurants or even one year, I received a new battery for my car. He was my first, and will remain, my favorite valentine. I know he loves and supports me day in and day out.

One of my dreams had always been to be a professional massage therapist, but I never had the confidence to pursue the necessary education and training. As I became more invested and competent with other healing modalities including Past Life Regression,

Hypnotherapy, Reiki and others, the more I knew I wanted to pursue massage. My friend and neighbor, Nancy, had gone through massage school and encouraged me to pursue it. Her encouragement supported my confidence in my ability to give it a try. I had quit school and training programs so many times before, I was worried this might end up the same.

"Could I actually finish something?" I kept asking myself. My boss was incredibly supportive and convinced corporate management to let me job-share so I would have the hours I needed for the massage program.

Of course working part-time raised financial concerns about being able to pay the rent and our other expenses. Although my relationship with Don was clearly on rocky ground, I still jumped at the chance for Shawn and I to move in with him. This would ease my financial burden and it seemed like a good idea for Shawn to have a man figure more prominently in his life. I didn't realize I was just getting into another situation with a partner with control issues who would expect submission from me.

Massage school was very challenging, Mastering anatomy, physiology, and kinesiology felt overwhelming. There were days I felt so frustrated, I cried and wanted to quit. "How could I possibly memorize the names and function of all the muscles in the body?" I wondered.

What was even more frustrating was Don quizzed me on my studies and seemed to understand and remember much more than I ever did. He expressed growing frustration that I just wasn't getting it.
My self esteem took another dive. I also decided to stop volunteering at the crisis clinic. School was so challenging and I just didn't have time to do both. Despite the hard work and frustration, something drove me forward. I was bound and determined to finally finish something in my life no matter how hard it was.

It had been two and a half years since Sam had been arrested. Finally his case came to trial and the prosecution called me to give testimony. As I sat on the bench outside the hall waiting for my name to be called, pictures of my past ran through my mind. I thought about all those times I wondered where he had disappeared to and the sleepless nights spent worrying and wondering, if and when, he was going to come home. The faces of our friends who still supported him and believed he didn't do it went through my mind. I figured the prosecution could do without my testimony and felt angry at getting dragged back into this horror. But I still wanted to protect Shawn. It was bad enough the authorities had subpoenaed me; I certainly didn't want to open the door to the possibility that Shawn would be questioned or involved.

As I sat on the bench running these ideas through my mind, a guard called my name. I got up and followed him into the courtroom. Looking around I saw a few people I recognized. I hadn't seen them in more than three years and they seemed like strangers to me.

Mentally I was in a completely different place than before. I felt like I was being misunderstood and judged for being a witness for the prosecution. How could anyone other than another witness understand this dilemma? Not only had I left Sam, but I had also abandoned this entire lifestyle months before the kidnapping and murder. But now I sat inside the court room waiting to be called up to the stand.

It seemed like an hour before they called me. I felt very uncomfortable and wanted nothing more than to just leave. I felt the negative energy being directed at me by Sam's friends and supporters. I was extremely angry at having to be involved in something I believed had nothing to do with me. When asked about my relationship with Sam, I answered he was just the biological father of my son and that was all. I saw him squirm slightly as if my words had cut him. There was hurt and a sense of betrayal in his eyes. I answered all their questions and was dismissed. I was pretty shaken up by the time it was over. All I could think of was getting out of there as soon as possible.

In what proved to be a very controversial decision, Sam was convicted of aggravated murder, first degree kidnapping and first degree rape of a child. The case remains controversial and my understanding is legal scholars and students include it as part of their studies. I am not qualified to evaluate the various discussions and legal arguments, but suffice it to say there were the usual accusations of circumstantial evidence, discrepancies between witness testimonies, the lack of aggressively pursuing alternate suspects, mishandling of evidence and the possibility the DNA evidence, so crucial to the case, was planted by the police or otherwise mishandled. (To this day Sam has asserted he is innocent and unfairly convicted. As for me, I don't know the truth and have no interest in arguing one side or the other.)

Following the trial, one of the defense attorneys called and asked if I would be a witness in their attempt to avert a death penalty sentence. I was shocked by my response. I told the attorney Sam was worth more to me and my son dead than alive. At least Shawn would be able to collect social security benefits. If Sam sat in prison for the rest of his life, we would receive no financial support and as taxpayers, we would be helping to pay the estimated $30,000 a year to house him. (This estimate is based on an Associated Press release dated November 26, 2007 for the State of Washington.)

I clearly still felt betrayed and had significant anger issues! The defense attorney quickly thanked me and hung up. Sam didn't get the death penalty; he was sentenced to life in prison with no parole. Looking back on it with my current perspective, I would willingly be a defense witness. No one deserves to die in this manner. I never wanted to see Sam again, but more than ten years later, mostly because of our son, I changed my mind.

A few months later Don and I decided to marry. I had vowed never to change my last name again after already changing it once when I married Jesse's father, Matt. However, we were leading a Christian life and he had a very public persona speaking to various churches and communities. I didn't want the hassle of arguing about it, so I caved in and changed my name. I told myself it really didn't matter in the bigger scheme of things and it was worth it to make him happy.

We planned a very small and intimate ceremony attended only by our children, two witnesses, and the minister of our church. We chose a natural setting along the waterfront on the beach. It was casual dress even though I dreamed of wearing a wedding dress since my first wedding was little more than vows exchanged in front of the justice of the peace. But it wasn't meant to be. We opted for a very casual and informal affair.

The night before our ceremony, Don came home completely drunk. He could hardly walk and was ranting and raving about how unhappy he was and how he was not worth marrying. He continued on about his failed marriage and was questioning how this union was going to work. He made quite the scene, getting louder and louder. The boys were in the other room playing and trying to ignore the chaos. I just wanted Don to be quiet. I told him we didn't have to get married and that sent him into a rage. He said he wasn't backing down now.

Every sense in my body told me to cancel the wedding right then and there; but I was afraid of what everyone would say. I didn't want to inconvenience anyone. I would have to call his daughters, the minister, and my family to explain we were postponing the wedding. This was too much for me to think about. The fear of where Shawn and I would go if I called off the wedding terrified me. We would have to move again and with my part-time income, how would we make it?

Don announced he was going to the store. I took his keys but he pushed me and got them back. I was shocked; he had never laid a hand on me before. I couldn't stop him so I called the police. They showed up in time and advised him to stay put. The police officer gave me the keys. Don slept outside in his truck that night. The next morning we were married.

Going to massage school proved to be the most difficult and challenging goal I had ever set for myself. I kept myself going by visualizing all the hard work paying off. I was ecstatic the day I walked out of the licensure office after passing my state board examination. I was now a Licensed Massage Practitioner. Now I could work less and be more accessible to my sons. I'd have more time and freedom to be involved in school functions and be there for Shawn when he came home from school each day.

Don and I decided to do a Christian radio program every Saturday. Soon after we began, Don expressed concerns about my individual segment of the show. I talked about how to be positive and how to manifest our heart's desire. It was upbeat and I was getting good feedback from listeners. But there was a problem. Don wrote scripts for me to follow but I liked going off script and adding a part of myself. Being told what to say took all the fun out of it, so not surprisingly, I quit doing the segment.

The relationship was a chaotic one. At one point, he insisted I get rid of my entire collection of pagan and healing books. I did as he asked, but not without feeling remorse and resenting the feeling of being controlled. This was an all too familiar pattern for me, denying my feelings because I wanted a relationship to work.

As time went on, I began to realize Don and I did not have a shared vision for our lives together. We were both very unhappy. Don drank obsessively and I used food and over-eating as a coping mechanism. I quit my job as a regional assistant. We moved to Olympia to be closer to my family who watched Shawn after school. I worked hard to get my healing practice established. I had also been accepted into a program at the Institute of Transpersonal Psychology with a focus on Dreams, Intuition and ESP.

Free of the fog of the drugs that had so influenced earlier parts of my life, my concentration improved. This was a welcome change as my studies required lots of reading, research and written papers. It seemed each time I wanted to work on my studies, Don created some sort of interfering chaos. I decided to work out of town at the ocean and in the rainforest one or two weekends a month. This helped me study and write papers in between clients.

WAKING UP TO MY TRUE SELF

Following the trauma of the terrorist attacks on the US on September 11, 2001, my life seemed to go into a free fall. I started looking deeper into my life realizing Don and I couldn't continue the course we were following. We both knew our life together was not working and changes needed to be made. Don told me almost every day he was leaving me, but never did. I was suspicious of the long hours he spent at work and how often he worked on projects with a co-worker. When I asked about it, he was defensive and said awful things about her. He created smoke screens in an attempt to divert my attention away from his indiscretions. I certainly had my suspicions, but didn't know anything for sure.

I needed to take some time out for myself to reflect on what would be the best thing to do in this situation. I attended a ten-day meditation retreat. Outside of massage school, it was one of the hardest things I had ever attempted. I woke up to a gong at 4 am and meditated almost unceasingly until going to bed at 9:30 pm. The only non-meditation time was a 90-minute lunch period and another brief break for a light supper in the evening. I planned my escape on the third day but ended up not going through with it. I stuck it out through the tenth day but didn't stay the last night which was part of the process. I was anxious to get home to Shawn. I came home feeling a lot clearer and with a plan of action. I didn't want my life to remain the same.

I was turning forty within the year and treasured a dream that by the time I reached this age I would be well on my way to becoming more of an advocate for women, supporting and empowering them to be the best they could be. I realized I needed to be an advocate for myself and make the changes that would lead to greater happiness for us all. My goal and life dreams were not going to manifest if I continued on this path with Don.

A few days after getting back from my retreat, things came to a head when Don showed up intoxicated at my office. He stood in the reception area yelling for me while I was in a treatment room with a client. I excused myself and went out into the reception area silently giving thanks that no other client was waiting there witnessing the scene. I rushed him out and prayed he didn't hurt anyone on his drive home. I was very embarrassed as I went back into the massage room to finish the treatment. Fortunately, my client took it lightly and with a sense of humor. I on the other hand, worried about him coming back, and about whether or not he made it home safely.

I was convinced more than ever things needed to change. I was determined to take control of my own destiny. I told him we were going to get divorced and asked him to move out for good. Immediately I changed back to my maiden name and vowed to never change it again. Since my dad didn't have any boys, I would be the one who would carry the name forward. I started to feel empowered again.

My biggest fear and concern was financial. Don never tired of telling me I couldn't make it on my own and would fall apart without him. I was pleasantly surprised the month after he had moved out, there was more money in the bank account then there had been for years. Spirit showed me I could do this on my own as long as I drew upon my connection to my source and maintained my faith. When we stay connected we are blessed in unknown and unexpected ways.

I filed the divorce papers, and we met about a month later in a parking lot. He signed the papers and I never saw him again. Several months later, I received a notice from Don's medical insurance carrier. I smiled when I read the letter and saw another woman listed with his last name. He had married his co-worker. My suspicions were correct; he was having an affair. I remember how disparagingly he had spoken of her. (This is not uncommon for someone involved in an affair to speak badly of their lover when confronted.)

Even though I continued to offer sessions of past life regressions, hypnotherapy and energy work with crystals and tuning forks, massage seemed to be taking most of my time. There were days I had to remind myself more than once that doing massage therapy was only temporary and I would eventually be able to help women in other ways. In the meantime, I started a weekly psychic support group where I led the group through meditations and a variety of techniques to develop and improve their intuition.

Before I knew it, my massage business grew exponentially and edged out most of my other healing modalities. I was extremely busy and found I couldn't say no to any of my clients. I held time in my schedule book for helping women and teaching psychic development classes, but received so many requests for massage sessions, it wasn't long before I stopped facilitating the psychic support group because I just didn't have time for it anymore. My busy massage practice also consumed any time I might have devoted to the women's shelter. I was completely focused on bringing in money to meet my expenses and to finance a few workshops and vacations. I wasn't quite aware of Divine Timing yet, so I pushed through my days and believed the more I worked, the faster I would get where I wanted to go.

Thoughts, about my encounter with the alien, pop into my head every now and then. He usually just stops by and says "hi" and lets me know he is in the area. One week he came into my mind for several days. I knew that if I wanted to know the name of a guide all I had to do was ask. So I decided I would ask my alien friend, "What is your name?" Nothing came to my mind so I let it go.

The same day, I asked for his name, a regular client came in for her appointment. Previously she and I had discussed ergonomics. When she arrived for her appointment she brought an ergonomic pen and instead of laying it on my desk, she set it up on its end. As soon as I saw it, I said it looked like a space ship. She responded, "Andy wants you to have this." Andy was her boyfriend at the time, but I knew my alien friend was giving me his name!

Shawn was almost 16 years old when he started asking me about Sam saying he might want to see him someday. My first thought was, "No, he is no longer a part of our lives." As a typical teenager, Shawn was experimenting with his independence, as all kids will, and started thinking he wanted to see his dad despite my obvious resistance. It took me some time, but eventually I came around to his way of thinking. I attempted to put myself in his shoes and tried to imagine how I would feel in the same situation. I knew myself well enough to know that I would resent my guardian parent and find a way to visit the incarcerated parent on my own.

It was important to me to show Shawn I always supported him, even if I didn't agree with his choices. I wanted to make sure he realized this. Eventually he would be old enough to make this decision on his own without my approval but was it really necessary to force him to wait? I was also concerned about Shawn perceiving me as the "bad guy". If he established a relationship with Sam, who in my experience was very adept at manipulation, I wanted Shawn to know I was on his side and he could count on me. I wanted my relationship with Shawn to be honest and solid.

I thought about it and debated back and forth with myself for quite some time before making the decision to re-establish contact with Sam as well as with his family. We had no contact with his family through the years, not even to exchange birthday or holiday cards. I tried to prepare Shawn by talking about manipulation and how a person might control a conversation or try to influence or create bias. I told him it was very important to stay neutral when talking to his father and encouraged him to keep the conversation focused on the present. I warned him about the possibility Sam would want to talk about why he was in prison. I emphasized the importance of staying neutral and staying focused on what was really important which in my mind, was not the crime, but instead was Shawn's relationship with his father. I explained to Shawn that Sam might want to talk about the case and focus on what he believed was unfair. This might be a way Sam would attempt to manipulate Shawn and win his approval. I didn't want Shawn to get sucked in and I told him so.

I admit I was also curious about Sam after all these years. I contacted his mother and told her we were interested in visiting him. She made sure we received the appropriate paperwork so we could arrange a visit. Sam was incarcerated at Washington State Penitentiary in Walla Walla at the time and as it turned out, we were never able to arrange a time for a visit. The timing was also complicated somewhat by the fact I decided I would like to see Sam first, to scope out the environment before taking Shawn to see him.

I was extremely busy with my business. I had more massage clients then I knew what to do with, but nevertheless felt restless and discontent. I was searching but not sure what I was even searching for. I had given up my addiction to drugs and continued to be very aware of my tendencies to eat when I was stressed, but didn't realize addictive tendencies were turning me into a workaholic. I defended my behavior with rationalizations that I needed to push myself and work as much as possible so I could afford everything I wanted for myself and Shawn's future while also being able to help Jesse. I was still paying child support to my ex-husband Matt, and giving Jesse additional money whenever he needed it. I wanted to take both boys to Disneyland and I did. I did what I could to make sure Shawn and I were part of Jesse's life including driving down to watch his basketball and football games whenever possible.

An opportunity for a vacation presented itself. It was the chance to take a week off and float down the Colorado River through the Grand Canyon, in springtime when the cacti were in bloom. I really wanted Shawn to come with me but he refused, saying it wouldn't be any fun. I knew there was no use in forcing him to do something he didn't want to do. We would both be miserable. I had tried unsuccessfully too many times to get him to go camping or hiking. We always ended up arguing the whole time.

I wanted to take some light reading with me on the trip. I went to the book store and very quickly "Healing with the Faeries" by Doreen Virtue, sparked an interest. I had never heard of Doreen, but having had a lifetime affinity with the faeries, decided it would be an easy read. I didn't allow myself to read it until I started my vacation. I couldn't wait to get into my tent each night and with the light of my little flashlight, read a little bit more. I resonated with everything she wrote about.

Returning home, I looked at her website and noted she was teaching a workshop called "Angel Therapy" scheduled in Laguna Beach just a few months away. This really resonated with me, although I couldn't fathom how I was going to be able to go. I'd have to take time off work and come up with the money for the workshop and the trip. Since I had just returned from a week vacation I knew it would be a challenge to pull this together. But I knew if spirit wanted me there, a way would open. I usually worked seven days a week, but I felt in my bones I would be there. I still don't know how I manifested it but I did. The adage "Where there's a will there's a way!" certainly holds true. I think the faeries thought I needed to go as well, because once I set the intention to go, I had a few clients who were happy to prepay for sessions which gave me enough money to pay the registration fee. I agreed to share a hotel room and also got a great deal on the airfare.

Everything happened smoothly; and indeed, attending this workshop changed my life. I remember sitting in the workshop with hundreds of other students hearing Doreen tell us our class was full of future teachers who would help many others by teaching them about the Angels. She looked many of us in the eyes that day as she said this. I know others resonated to the message in the same way I did, because many of them have, in fact, changed their lives and are channeling angel messages and teaching people to connect with angels today. I started doing angel readings for people as soon as I returned; and soon was getting at least several requests each week. I was opening up to the Universe and my intuition more than ever before.

I liked to drive up to Port Townsend, a quaint little Victorian style town between the Olympic Mountains and the Puget Sound for a day trip to visit "Phoenix

Rising", the best metaphysical book store in the North West, with the largest inventory of statues, and crystals of all shapes and sizes, along with lots of other goodies.

I spent hours in the store looking at everything and dreaming of owning one of the beautiful crystal balls the store had for sale. I also had a vision of actually doing readings there but felt too intimidated and inexperienced at first, to inquire about it. I would leave my browsing sessions knowing maybe someday I would have the gumption to check it out. One day, I got the nerve to call the store and ask if they might need a reader. As luck would have it, the owner of the store, told me she was looking for someone who could fill in occasionally. We made a date for me to come up and give her a reading.

I was very nervous as I drove towards the store that morning. The drive along the canal was a peaceful and beautiful one as I followed the Puget Sound on the twisting and turning road glimpsing the mountains in the distance. I arrived at the store about 20 minutes early and parked across the street. I was nervous and excited at the same time. I kept telling myself to let go of any attachment to getting the job. It would be good practice for me, if nothing else. I took a deep breath and walked into the store. The owner told me to go up stairs and set up in the room. I didn't have anything to set up, so I walked up the stairs with just me.

I sat on one side of the small table waiting for the owner. She came in and sat across from me. I took her hands in mine and asked for our guides and angels to come in and help with the reading, and gave thanks for any help given. She listened as I shared the information I was receiving. When it was over, I sat waiting for her to say something. She smiled at me and said I could fill in for another reader who needed some time off. I thought I was going to jump out of my skin. I was so excited.
As she got up, she asked me if I used any sort of oracle to help with my readings. I hadn't even thought about it. She suggested people like having something in front of them to look at, and it is sometimes easier for them to accept the information when an oracle is used. From that day forward I started using my oracle cards. I always save them for the last few minutes of the reading to confirm what I have already received from spirit. I've learned some people do have the expectation of an oracle being involved in a reading. Some clients have even asked me "when are you going to get the cards out?"

It was finally time to make good on my commitment to Shawn to visit his father in prison. The first time, I was surprised at the heavy energy I felt as I drove past the check-in speaker. I took a few deep breaths because the air felt so thick. Part of the energy was probably related to my own anxiety; after all I hadn't seen Sam for over 10 years.

I checked in at the desk. They checked my ID, took my car key, had me walk through a metal detector, stamped the back of my hand and gave me the ok to move through a series of electronic doors. I continued down a long hallway to yet another door that opened into a big open room with a guard who greeted me. The guard instructed me to wave my stamped hand under a light and then directed me to another guard at a big desk across the room.

The room was filled with small tables big enough for four people to sit around them. There were bigger tables at the back of the room with a sign designating it as a family area. Vending machines lined one of the walls. Along another wall was a microwave, and condiment bar. There were shelves of games and puzzles. There were paintings on the wall I assumed had been painted by the prisoners. The guard instructed me to sit at table number seven. I was glad; seven had been my favorite number for as long as I could remember. I sat down in a chair and waited. The guard approached and told me I needed to move. I didn't understand what he meant and looked at him. He pointed to the yellow tape on the back of the chair. I was sitting in the chair designated for an inmate. I got up and moved to the chair next to it.

As I looked around I noticed yellow tape on one chair at each table. I couldn't help but stare at the other inmates visiting with their guests. Some of them wore tan coveralls and others were in plain street clothes. I found myself wondering why they were there. What could they have possibly done? Many of them looked just like the average Joe on the street while others looked like they could have committed almost any crime imaginable. I was surprised at the mix of energies and diversity in physical appearances. I noticed a piece of paper on the table and picked it up and started reading. It was the rules of conduct. We were not to touch one another under the table, kiss for longer than 2 seconds, only 5 people at the vending machines at a time, no talking to the people at the other tables, and when the guards did an inmate count, we were to stay seated.

I watched visitors come in and sit down. An inmate would show up shortly afterwards. I started wondering why Sam had not made an appearance yet. As if the guard was reading my mind, he came over and explained Sam was in band practice and was putting his equipment away. He would be out soon. I thanked him for letting me know. It hadn't occurred to me Sam would be in a band in this of all places. I smiled at the thought of it. I remembered all the times we were supposed to be somewhere but he was late because of band practice. I had spent a lot of time waiting on him. I also remembered shortly after one of his arrests when I talked with him, he sounded more upbeat and actually sounded better than I remembered him in the outside world. I asked him about this several times. He assured me he was happier outside prison walls than inside, but there were times I wasn't convinced.

I waited patiently, silently asking Saint Germain and Archangel Michael to protect me and ward off any negative and dark energy. I intently watched the windowed door where the inmates entered the big visiting area. He was there waiting to enter the same room as me. He looked the same as I remembered him. He smiled and waved at me and I waved back. I felt emotion welling up inside. Only moments before I felt like a brick – hard and as if nothing could get through to me. My emotions changed from sadness to happiness and back to sadness again. How could a life be so wasted as this? How could someone take the life of a child? Did he? Was he guilty? If he was innocent, how could it be that he would spend the rest of his life this way? None of it seemed fair.

I stood up as he approached. He reached out but then stopped himself asking me, if it was alright to hug. I said, "Of course!" We hugged and for just a split second it seemed like old times, before all the chaos. Much of the negativity seemed to dissolve. We sat down and he continued to look at me. He said, "You look good! Life has done you well." I said, "Same to you, prison has done you well!" Unfortunately, this was an old habit, trying to make a joke when I had no idea what to say. Sam laughed. He always had a great sense of humor.

I admitted I was there to check things out before bringing Shawn in for a visit. He was grateful I was agreeing to let Shawn come. He started to talk about the trial and the unfairness of it all and I stopped him. I told him I didn't want to talk about it because it wasn't why I had come. I explained to him it was the last thing I wanted to talk about and asked him to not discuss it with Shawn. I told him I was only interested in talking about the present and did not want to dig up the past, what had happened, or the perceived injustice.

We spent most of the day together talking about life, and metaphysical thoughts and ideas. He wanted to know what we had been up to in the past 10 years so I gave him the highlights. I asked him to tell me about a typical day for him in prison. He was reading the bible for the fifth time and practiced playing his bass guitar once a week with a few guys. He was making ink art and writing in a journal. He told me he worked five days a week in the print shop making business cards and working on other print jobs for some of the businesses in town. He was paid about 30 cents a day which he spent buying personal supplies and food such as Top Ramen which he ate when he was hungry between meal times. (From my understanding most of the jobs the inmates used to have are no longer done by inmates because of budget cuts and security reasons. In my last communication with Sam, he reported he was playing in two bands each week.) As I left that day, I felt comfortable about bringing Shawn for a visit.

Shawn grew into a handsome young man and had just gotten his driver's license. My older son Jesse and his girlfriend moved in with us. For the most part the kids were independent and I was a lot freer to venture off on the weekends.

One weekend a hiking buddy and I headed up towards Steven's Pass to go camping. We arrived at the campsite early to set up so we wouldn't have to come back from our hike tired with lots to do. We could fix our dinner; relax by the fire, and go to sleep. We expected to be hungry from the strenuous hiking and fresh mountain air. We set up our camp and secured our food in the bear box down the trail from our camp. We took off along the road until we found the trail head leading towards the river.

The trail curved in and around giant fallen trees. I could hear the river in the very near distance. It was raging loud and clear. There were trees with moss hanging down from the branches as if the elves had decorated for a celebration. The aroma of pine wafted through the air and tree roots grabbed playfully at my feet as I carefully stepped over them. The path was full of magic. My friend was a fast hiker so by this time I was panting and huffing trying hard to keep up with him. I liked being challenged. Among my female hiking friends it was I who challenged them, so I was thrilled to have this guy who challenged me to push beyond my usual limits. The downside was I couldn't stop to observe my surroundings too long before he was out of sight and I had to hurry to catch up.

I looked up into the hill and wondered what was watching us. Was it a cougar? Was it a bear? Was it a tiny little animal such as a squirrel gathering supplies for winter? As we started our descent and turned towards the sound of the river, I noticed there were washed out areas of brush with a chaotic assortment of giant trees, some sprawled haphazardly on the ground. It was as if the river had overflowed its banks in a torrent, tearing a path through the forest, tossing trees aside in its wake leaving a domino of trees dotting the bank as far as I could see.

The water was raging as we stepped upon a newly built wooden bridge suspended by thick heavy metal cord. I looked up river and imagined a wall of water coming towards us. I quickened my pace and at the same time watched my every step because the boards were slippery under my feet. I could hear my heart pounding in my ears, temporarily masking the roar of the river. My heart raced and yet I couldn't help but stop once again and look down at the river. Where would the river take me? Where would I go? I turned and looked up again. A feeling of fear rose within me at the thought of being immersed under the water. I was already feeling inundated by the explosive roar of the moving water all around me. At the same time, I felt exhilaration as if the force of the wilderness was cleansing my soul.

I stepped off the bridge and walked in between two uprooted trees. The roots were still intact with deep clumps of soil holding the entire infrastructure that reached up into the sky in a circular pattern as high as twelve feet. I could smell the strong and pungent odor of the soil. I took several deep breaths and enveloped my senses with the smell and experience. I tried to keep a sharp outlook ahead so I wouldn't trip over any roots or rocks. In some areas, one wrong step could have sent me tumbling down towards the river.

As we climbed, I noticed all the faerie dwellings and animal trails. We walked over smaller bridges built over little waterfalls flowing towards the raging river down below. Higher up in the alpine forest, the trail led to a narrow path with a ledge on one side looking down to the valley below. There were snow capped peaks set above the backdrop of the river bank on the other side. The view was breath-taking. We stopped for a rest and a snack. The other side of the trail was a thick bramble of low growing plants climbing steadily uphill. I felt an incredible deep peace as we sat just taking it all in.

The sun was dipping into the western sky so we begrudgingly got up and headed back wishing we had not taken so much time setting up the camp before starting our hike. It didn't take as long to get back as we were heading steadily downhill. I was thankful I had my trekking poles with me. Even though my ankle seemed to be holding up and rather enjoying this hike, it was reassuring I had a cane along with me to act as an extra leg if I needed it for support. I knew my ankle would become a bit touchier as the day wore on. My ankle was always a little hesitant in the beginning, and after exercising for an extended time and taking a break it would become stiff. At such times I often kidded with my friends saying rigor mortis was setting in. When I started moving again, the exercise would free it up a little. I had not let my ankle injury stop me yet and didn't plan for it to stop me anytime in the future.

I was relieved when the roaring of the river grew louder indicating we were getting closer to our campsite. We climbed off the ridge above the river and the forest grew quiet. The forest had quickly turned into a landscape of shadows. I could hear my heart beating as if it would come out of my chest. Our footsteps echoed and I started wondering again what was watching us. I smiled to myself and thought of how whatever was watching, would certainly be able to get closer to us because of decreasing daylight. We got to the bridge and I didn't take any time to get across. I knew what was down the river and I knew what was coming towards us. I kept my eyes focused on the other side of the river. There was a red hue in the sky as the sun disappeared behind the hill top. We didn't have much farther to go and didn't need to get our head lamps out, as we would make it back into the camp ground before dark.

As we continued down the path, I felt this overwhelming feeling something was very near and that we were being watched. I thought of a cougar because they were quiet, sleek and stealthy. I walked faster keeping right in tune with my hiking buddy's footsteps. The space between us could not have been more than an inch. I was keeping as close to him as possible without touching him. I didn't want him to think I was scared. We were both very silent, not like earlier when we were pointing out areas of interest and talking about everything. Our only thought was to get back to camp. I was even more relieved when I saw the trail head and up further I could see the bathrooms. We made a stop knowing the bathrooms were a distance from our camp site and we wouldn't want to walk back here later. Our camp was still about quarter of a mile down the road and in the dark and cold, even with a head lamp, it wasn't something I wanted to do later.

We got to the camp site, built a small fire and lit the kerosene stove to heat our soup. It was cold and I was tired. Since we didn't collect much fire wood before we left, the fire was small and didn't really warm us through. We decided we might as well go to bed. We dressed in layers with all the clothes we brought. I used a pair of pants as a pillow since I had forgotten to bring mine. I was pretty tired and grumpy and not having my pillow made it worse. I told myself there was nothing I could do. I would survive.

We positioned ourselves back to back to keep warm. As I lay there I was aware of how I was getting myself all worked up. I couldn't believe I had forgotten my pillow. I took deep breaths and told myself it really didn't matter in the big scheme of things. I thought about how cold I felt. I visualized being in a very warm room. The coldness was just in my imagination. I continued breathing deep relaxing breaths and exhaling the frustration I was feeling for not being as organized as I would have liked to have been.

There were meshed windows on each side of this little three-man tent and as my hiking buddy put the flaps down I could still see through them into the darkness outside. I closed my eyes once again and this time started drifting off. I am not sure how long I was out when I got a sense I was dreaming, but still very aware of my surroundings. I felt something from the outside coming closer. My body was paralyzed, and as much as I tried, I couldn't move. I wanted to wake up and move as I continued to sense something coming towards me. The thought of a bear ran through my mind.

I remembered the bear boxes where we put our food earlier. All of a sudden the fear of bears which I had experienced earlier in the day disappeared. Instead, as I lay there it was as if I was being invited by the very bears I feared, to bond and become one with them. As I surrendered to this thought, I felt the very essence of my being merge with what I can only describe as the Great Bear Spirit. I could feel the power of bear and a great GROWL from deep inside me made its way forth as I GROOOOOWWWWLEEED with a sound I had never heard before. I came to with my buddy screaming "AAAWWW" as he crawled frantically towards the door, unzipping the tent to get away. When I realized the sound had come from me, I lay laughing uncontrollably with excitement. I had shape shifted into a bear. Try as I might, I couldn't stop laughing.

My hiking buddy was furious as he had been awakened from a sound sleep, convinced a bear had entered the tent and was getting ready to devour him. He didn't find it funny at all to be awakened by the person beside him growling. I scared him to death. My laughing didn't help matters. I couldn't seem to stop and the more I laughed, the angrier he got. He told me I was possessed and said I sounded just like a bear. I told him I shape shifted but it wasn't on purpose. He wasn't a believer and I laughed even more at the idea he thought I was possessed.

His words and attitude did not diminish my happiness. I had just experienced a special moment with my bear totem. Bear had been my totem for many years. This experience would remain a fond memory etched in my heart and in my mind. As we settled back down to sleep, I tried really hard to be quiet but occasionally would burst into hysterical laughter until tears rolled down my face. I think this was definitely influential in the demise of our hiking trips together.

I continued to learn as much as I could about anything involving metaphysics. Any class or workshop that remotely piqued my interest, I signed up for and figured a way to take it. I traveled back to Laguna Beach in California a few times and I even flew to Kona, Hawaii several times to take more classes. I participated in classes over the internet and by teleconference. I even took classes on nutrition and the raw food way of life. I couldn't get enough.

As I learned more and more about my own intuition and about helping others follow theirs, I received more communications from those who had passed over. Some were deceased loved ones of mine and some I didn't know. It started happening more and more often that I would receive a message with a directive to give a message to someone.

Especially during the holidays I was inundated with messages. This made me feel very uncomfortable. I had said all along I wasn't interested in mediumship – this art of communicating with the dead. I was more than content talking with my guides and angels; this was good enough for me. I felt I didn't know enough to really help anyone and decided it was time to get a better and deeper understanding of mediumship. Then maybe I could help others using this psychic gift. I registered for a mediumship class in Kona and made arrangements to share a hotel room to keep my expenses down.

My roommate suggested it would be fun to swim with dolphins and it sounded like a great idea to me. We connected with a woman living on the island who agreed to include us in a trip she was planning. The trip was scheduled for the first morning I was on the island.

Truthfully, I wasn't quite prepared to head out on a boat the day after I had just flown in the night before. I have a tendency to get motion sickness quite easily and didn't think about asking my guides and angels to help me with it. The further out in the water we were, the more the boat rocked. I would have liked to get to know the others on the boat but I was pre-occupied with just trying to hold it together. I was thankful when we stopped and I was able to get into the water and swim.

There were a couple of dolphins swimming near me in the water when all of a sudden I was in the midst of a whole pod of wild dolphins. They were all around us. I felt very blessed. The water was filled with fun and happy energy. It was an experience I will never forget. Little did I know that a couple of years later, six of the nine people on the boat that day would work as advisors for the same psychic hot-line as spiritual and psychic advisors.

One thing on my wish list was having a crystal ball of my own. This dream manifested several months later when I was in Port Townsend doing readings at the metaphysical bookstore. I was admiring the crystal balls as I did each time I was in the store and mentioned to the owner, my desire to have one of my own someday. I had been working there for several years, and no doubt those who worked at the store had seen me drool over them many times. The owner offered to let me choose one and make monthly payments. I was so grateful she trusted me with such a valuable object and worthwhile investment. I am the proud owner of a Lemurian Crystal ball.

Several months after my initial trip to see Sam in prison, Shawn mentioned he was ready to go visit. I reminded him of our previous conversations about the subtle dynamics of persuasion and covert manipulation. I wanted him to approach this visit with his father without expectations or attachments to the outcome. At the same time, I wanted him to pay attention to his feelings both during and after the visit. I didn't want Shawn to feel sorry for Sam or start believing he was too nice to have been accused of the crime for which he was serving a life sentence.

Even though Sam maintains his innocence, to this day, it is also true he has a history as a sexual offender. And although I loved him and certainly fell under the spell of his charms, I felt manipulated, demeaned and controlled by him during our time together. He himself was a victim of violence and abuse. But nevertheless, in my experience he was capable of exhibiting some of the classic signs of abusers including being a master manipulator. I didn't want Shawn to be negatively influenced or harmed. I wanted Shawn to listen to his inner self and learn to trust his intuition.

Fortunately the visit went off without a hitch. Sam was very happy to see Shawn and we visited for several hours. Sam was also on his best behavior and complied with my request to keep the conversation light and in the present.

Winter came and so did an opportunity to house sit for a couple of months in a wonderful brick house, built in the sixties on Lake Stevens. The house had been empty for more than a year following the passing of the couple who had lived there. The antique furniture remained as it had been arranged for years. I could sense a lot of paranormal activity here. The house had a charm I couldn't resist, so I took the owners up on their offer and moved in. I was able to communicate with lots of my guides and angels as well as others who inhabited the house since it had been empty for so long. (In my experience, entities have a tendency to settle into houses that remain empty for a long time.) I asked them to leave and go to the light and also did a lot of clearing in the process. It was the first time I had ever lived alone (well alone in the sense without humans) in my entire life and I was thrilled. I had a magnificent view of the lake and flowers galore in the huge manicured yard.

For several years I had been working as an advisor for a psychic hotline. The owner worked tirelessly making our site a reliable and a safe harbor for clients to trust. The process for being accepted onto the site as a reader was in-depth and detailed, designed to attract only the experienced and dedicated to this field. As an expansion of the site and in an attempt to create a home for educational and inspiration talk shows, the owner developed a sister site, 12Radio.com. It was a win / win situation. The advisors turned radio hosts had the opportunity to teach, inspire, offer free readings, live their passion, and even indulge their desire for a bit of public celebrity. Listeners benefit by having a safe place to come and listen to our shows where they can feel inspired and uplifted while they are also learning more about a variety of topics including intuition, angels, astrology, metaphysics and so much more. I was excited about doing radio. I hadn't done it since early

2000 and was ready to get my feet wet again. I loved looking out the window over the lake while doing my show.

My time house-sitting came to an end and I moved back to Olympia. I spent my time doing in-person readings, taking calls on the psychic hotline, and doing massage and energy work for my long-time clients. Most had been with me for more than ten years. I wasn't taking any new massage clients and had long since stopped marketing or advertising my massage business. I focused on my intuitive work holding onto my dream of helping other women become the best they could be by inspiring and motivating them to live closer to their passions and make positive changes in their lives.

I traveled up to Port Townsend once a month to do readings at the bookstore and also had clients in Seattle. I continued doing my radio show, "Groovy Green Goddess" and enjoyed just living life in the present moment. Everything was going pretty well. A year went by and I starting feeling restless once again. When I moved down to Olympia ten years before, I knew it would not be permanent. I always had the feeling I needed to travel and let my wings soar. My sons were grown and living their own lives. They both are responsible adults and good kids and that is more than enough reason to give thanks.

I settled back into my life in Olympia working with clients, doing readings and teaching classes on intuition, eating healthy and creating a wholesome life. It was nice to be in my hometown but something kept calling me beyond. So I continued to take out-of-town jobs and accept opportunities to travel whenever I could.

It was the middle of July when I rented a small cottage, for a month in Port Townsend. I wanted to break out of my normal everyday routine to think about what adventures life might have in store for me. I had a few options including moving to New Mexico, staying in Port Townsend, returning to Olympia or something yet unknown. I was open to whatever could be and I had a month to let it unfold. With my sons growing and living on their own, I felt free to spread my wings and was open to move wherever spirit would take me.

Most mornings, I walked down to a park near my cottage and followed a trail down to the water. Some mornings I sat on a log and stared out into the water.

As I meditated, I could feel the gentle mermaid energy lift me and prepare me for whatever the day would bring. I often pondered whether or not mermaids really did live and swim in the ocean or if the idea of them is really our collective thoughts coalescing as mermaid energy, from which we draw good intentions and beliefs. In the end it really doesn't matter; but I personally believe there are mermaids among us. I was also very drawn to octopi in the Puget Sound and consider them to be included among my totems. I knew the octopus and mermaids were friends, but until recently had not had the opportunity to get to know the mermaids in the same way I hung out with the faeries.

Shortly before my birthday in August, I was in Tacoma hanging out with a girlfriend named Karen. We celebrated my birthday with lunch at a local restaurant and brewery located on the waterfront. During lunch I told Karen about a recent experience I had in Port Townsend. I was there doing intuitive readings at the book store. During a break, I visited a friend who worked nearby at a specialty tea shop. While she was with a customer I had the chance to look around the shop. I became infatuated with mermaids hanging from the ceiling. They were crafted individually by a local artist from rawhide and decorated with beads and sea shells. I fell in love with them and couldn't help thinking not only did I want one, but that many other people would love them as well.

Seeing the mermaids got my creative juices flowing and I imagined smaller versions of these original treasures. I contacted the artist and several weeks later we connected over a pot of Earl Grey tea. I did an intuitive reading for her which included what I saw for her future (which has since come true). In exchange she gave me a beautiful 12-inch mermaid adorned with beads and seashells. To this day it is one of my prized and beloved possessions.

As Karen and I ate our lunch and enjoyed the Tacoma sunshine, I continued my stories about the mermaids, telling Karen about my latest experiences and how they were showing up in all sorts of unexpected circumstances. I was having a ball! Afterwards, we walked along the water and found a small section of logs and a patch of sand great for sitting. As we were hanging out, we noticed a bright pink object along the water line. Karen walked over, picked it up and said, "This is surely for you, Lacey". It was a little doll with long pink hair. Her two legs were very close together as if she was ready to transform into a mermaid if she went into the water. Karen and I both laughed in delight. The timing was perfect!

One day I had an opportunity to visit the San Juan Islands. As I was riding the ferry towards the islands, I felt an excitement I couldn't explain. I saw the islands off in the distance and felt an instant connection. It was as if I had returned from a long absence. I didn't want to leave. I stayed for a few days exploring the islands.

One amazing thing after another quickly occurred and I felt I was receiving all these gifts for just being there. I decided I was going to move to the island and trusted it would happen, if it was meant to be.

I walked into the Afterglow Spa at Roche Harbor Resort, and even though it was the end of the tourist season, they offered me a job. I moved into an old rustic house right on the bay where I could see the water every day.

At night when the tide was in, I could hear the crashing and frolicking of mermaids and sea lions. There was a black fox residing in the neighborhood who visited frequently. The happy chirping and singing of birds every morning were especially delightful. At times I could hardly contain my happiness. I felt so full of gratitude every day.

The next step in my plan was to find a place in Friday Harbor where I could do intuitive readings. Someone directed me to another gal who mentioned a store called Mystical Mermaid (of course). When I called the store, I was greeted by a very cheerful younger man's voice. I introduced myself and told him I was looking for a place to do intuitive readings. The immediate rapport I felt on the phone had me jumping up and down with expectation and excitement. I knew he was just as excited. He and his wife had just put out feelers to find a reader for their store. They bought the store several months before to fulfill their dream to get out of the city and raise their four children closer to nature. They bought the store and directed its focus towards metaphysics with lots of mermaid trinkets.

I had found my new home. I moved to the islands with a primary goal of writing, thinking there was no way I would be able to distract myself with the busyness that usually occupied my time and energy. This was an island and there wasn't much to do. I thought I'd be forced to write because there wouldn't be much to keep me distracted. Before I knew it, I was doing readings at the Mystical Mermaid, and working four days a week doing massage at the spa in Roche Harbor. I was hiking, writing and even helping my roommate with his business. (One of my stories was published in "Mermaids 101 by Doreen Virtue.)

My addiction to work and keeping busy moved with me to the islands and was in full swing. It didn't take long before I completely booked my time, working seven days a week with little opportunity for time off. I thought about a bumper sticker a friend displayed on her car, "Retired from the rat race, still trying to kill the rat!" I still hadn't learned to slow down.

I loved hiking, but the old injury to my leg still caused considerable pain and sometimes interfered with my love of outdoor activity. Reluctantly I went to have it looked at. The prognosis wasn't good. I remember that day as I listened to the doctor explain in detail everything he recommended be done. I kept thinking "It might just be simpler to amputate and be done with it."

The doctor recommended procedures to straighten my leg which would require breaking the tibia and surgery involving the fibula as well. Potentially, the surgery could compromise my knee function. Recovery would take 12-16 weeks and maybe more. During the healing process I would not be able to put any weight on my leg at all, but in the end the leg should heal and be stronger than before.

After that recovery I would then move on to the next procedure of replacing my ankle. This would require additional surgery and another 12-16 weeks of recovery with no weight bearing on my leg. If everything healed as planned, I would then need extensive rehabilitation.

I tried to stay open to all the options including the most radical, amputation above the knee. This option was certainly quick and efficient and frankly, was the cheapest and less time consuming of all. I had recently seen a banner on Facebook of a little girl with a missing leg and a grown man with a false leg who were running down a track. It wasn't too hard for me to imagine. I would survive if this was the option I chose. I started wondering about how I would feel about pedicures. I wondered, "Will I get a deal of fifty percent off?"

I felt frustrated with the whole idea of replacing the ankle. It was complicated and certainly not as easy as I had imagined it could be. This was a call to action and a reminder of the vow I made to myself to identify and use natural therapies to treat my leg and avoid more invasive procedures or the radical idea of losing a part of my leg for good. I knew a lot about natural remedies and complementary medicine and had faith I could deal with the challenge before me.

I thanked the doctor and left the office. As I walked out into the parking lot, I felt a spring in my step and an energy surrounding my ankle. I was kind of tripping because it was as if I was being shown I didn't have to be totally reliant upon modern or western medicine. The human race has always relied on natural remedies and alternative healing modalities which have helped mankind get this far, pretty much in one piece. The world is full of stories of people who have done what seems impossible. We hear about miracles every day. These stories along with my own miraculous experience, keep me believing that anything is possible.

The discussion with the doctor marked this day as a wake-up call to action. I knew I had to be totally honest with myself. If there was going to be healing on any level, it would have to start from within. I knew this unequivocally. It is up to us to believe in ourselves. We have to be optimistic about what the future will bring. I knew I could do things immediately, like massage my leg, which would help my body work more efficiently.

From that day forward I sent love and healing thoughts not only to myself but to others, on a daily basis. I pursued and was persistent with using energy and body work focusing on my leg. My leg still gives me pain almost every day, but I consider it a gentle reminder to take care of myself like a precious jewel. When I take the time to attend to my body and "polish" it as a valuable treasure, my ankle responds accordingly.

Every part of my body responds with appreciation to positive thoughts. I smile when people talk about having an Achilles heel because I know; I have my own Achilles ankle.

It is so easy to get lost in the shuffle of every day events and to prioritize everyone else over ourselves. How often are we the last person in line? Instead of spending time on activities we say we value, like exercise, walking, eating right, meditating, and staying in the present moment (just to name a few) we distract ourselves with other less rewarding choices. The secret is to ask our bodies what they need. Yes our bodies will answer us if we only slow down and ask. When we pay closer attention to what our bodies want to communicate with us, it makes for an easier time moving through life.

There are many ways to do this. One way is to make sure you get outside in nature away from man-made noise. For example going somewhere you can hear a stream trickle or a river roar as you walk beside it. Walk in a meadow where you hear the birds chirping their happy songs. Sit among the flowers and listen for the bees buzzing nearby. Sitting or walking in places of solitude and beauty also help. When we put off getting outside or taking some quiet moments of respite, we desensitize ourselves and find it more difficult to hear what our bodies are communicating to us. There are times when we are only aware of the pain and the discomfort and we become depressed. That's when we need to take action and make changes. We can make positive changes like getting more exercise or giving up a bad habit like smoking or overeating. Everything begins with just one step.

Drinking plenty of water is vital. Our bodies are made up of over 70% water and when we are not hydrating ourselves adequately, we are not able to hear what our bodies are trying to tell us. Breathing is another important aspect of listening to what our bodies are telling us. Taking the time to breathe by taking long deep breaths is helpful. On the exhale, focus on releasing ideas or thoughts that seem to be clogging up your mind. Let them flow out with every breath.

The most important thing is to take the time to tune into your body – every day! Listen to what it is saying and what it is revealing about your mental state. Remember Rome wasn't built in a day; be patient with yourself. Form a daily habit of sitting and listening to your body. When your shoulder is hurting, stop and ask it, "What do I need to know?" Be open to the message. It could be as simple as "Quit doing what you are doing because it is straining me!" Maybe it is asking you, "Please stretch me before you start to use me." Often the messages will be about getting more exercise and eating healthier foods.

Our bodies are quick and clear communicators when we are in stressful situations. For example, when I drove down the driveway towards the Sanctuary, my body tightened and I would start to get a headache. After asking my body why it was doing this, I heard the message; I needed to move on, that this was no longer the place for me. The surroundings were too harsh and in order to live in more harmony, I needed to move. It took several months and many synchronistic events to get me to finally take action and move on, as I described earlier.

Change is never easy but it is often necessary for the well-being of our bodies, mind and spirit. It's sometimes necessary to do what seems risky in order to initiate change in the way we are doing things and living our lives. We can facilitate the smoothness of transitions by having faith and keeping a positive frame of mind. It is "stinkin' thinkin" that creates challenge and frustration on our journey to the new. Indulging in negative thinking makes it easier to not follow through with what our hearts are telling us. It is the belief in ourselves that will make the difference. Prior conditioning sets the tone for whether or not we believe we can do something. Embrace the motto, "Fake it till you make it." It works. Better yet, "Faith it until you Make it". Act as if something has happened or is already true for you.

I began my journey of recovery and change by writing positive affirmations on index cards or sticky notes and carrying them around with me in my pocket for easy access throughout the day. They reminded me of ideas

I wanted to believe and attitudes I wanted to reinforce. If you really want to make a difference quickly, record some positive affirmations in your own voice and listen to them over and over; especially during times you are tempted to lean towards the negative. The more we practice, the more automatic and natural this becomes. It is important when faced with a negative situation that we turn to, and encourage ourselves, with positive affirmations and tap into our stored resources of positivity. Be like a squirrel stashing away nuts in the winter, and build your stash of positive influences.

As an avid hiker throughout my life, I have been fortunate to have some very good times in which my injured leg and ankle were not a concern. However, I've noticed as my diet fluctuates, so does my leg. When I eat dairy, or foods with wheat, gluten, and of course sugar, my joints become inflamed. My ankle swells and becomes sensitive. I believe this is the response of an overgrowth of yeast which contributes to inflammation within the body. I learned if I wanted to continue my hiking, I needed to avoid these food products.

The choice and responsibility is always ours when it comes to our health. Health care professionals and western medicine have a lot to offer in terms of diagnosis and helping us understand the dis-ease we may be manifesting. But ultimately treatment choices are ours to carefully consider.

I CAN SEE CLEARLY NOW

One day after finishing up a day of intuitive readings in Port Townsend, I headed back to my cottage in the San Juan Islands. My commute included a ferry ride and a forty-five minute drive to a second ferry which would take me home. The ferry was loading and people were walking on. I didn't get there in time to walk on with the foot passengers so I waited for the cars to load.

Afterwards, I got the signal it was my turn to walk onto the deck. A crow swooped down grazing my head. One of the ferry attendants saw it and we looked at each other in surprise. I smiled even more knowing the crow was greeting me. The crow has always shown up during major turning points in my life.

I quickly forgot about the crow as I became absorbed with my thoughts. The ferry landed and I hurried off with the other foot traffic. I walked quickly to my parked truck hoping to take off before the cars started to off load from the ferry. I still had a long drive to the second ferry and was hoping to have enough time to grab some groceries on the way.

I was pleased when I arrived at the Anacortes ferry dock with a half hour to spare. I sat in the truck writing when I heard a thud on the roof of the truck. I looked behind me into the bed and didn't see anything. I turned back towards the front of the truck just in time to see a crow fly over the roof directly in front of me, swooping down against the windshield and fly away cawing. I was thrilled – two crows in one day or maybe it was the same crow following me. I humorously and lovingly felt gratitude for the acknowledgment of my crow guide. Since silly things like this are always happening with signs and acknowledgment from our furry or feathered friends, I again didn't think too much of it.

Magic happens all around us. The secret is to be open to it. To believe in it and the Universe opens up and shows you through signs that you are not alone and that a God of your understanding is always near. It's when we are focused too much on the bad things and not willing to ask for help that we miss the golden nuggets called opportunities to point us in the direction for our highest good.

The next day I walked along the marina to the spa. A row of small trees lined the sidewalk along the water. I noticed a crow directly in front of me, up in one of the small tree tops. I looked up as I got closer to him and he started cawing. As I passed the tree, he flew and landed on a branch on the next tree in front of me and cawed. We locked eyes, as I walked towards him. This dance continued with him skipping from tree to tree as I walked. He continued to caw until I turned away to cross the street. It dawned on me as I walked away, there was major change coming. Usually when the crows spend this much time getting my attention it was right before a major decision to "Jump!" whether I saw a net or not. (Usually I don't see a net until after I have already jumped. Some call this faith.) It is about having faith the Universe will provide.

The crow in mystical writings is symbolically linked with Laws of the Universe and specifically to truth. It helps establish what truth is, especially in changing circumstances and helps us open to new understanding. The spirit of the crow shows up to alert us that change, in accordance with the laws of the universe, is about to happen. As I walked into the spa, I thought to myself there had been enough change taking place, so I had no idea what the crow was foretelling.

That evening I had another epiphany. A few months before when I decided to move into Friday Harbor, instead of living out in the country near Roche Harbor, I experienced some negativity from others regarding my line of work. I had looked at a few cottages in town and filled out applications for a couple of them. One was a little more than I wanted to pay for rent, so I turned it down. I found another which was very nice and affordable. When I filled out my application, I wrote down I was self employed as an intuitive advisor. I also included some excellent references from people on the island. The owner looked at it and asked me why I would list intuitive advisor as my occupation when the people on the island were considered to be very traditional and conservative? I explained doing readings was the source of my income and I wasn't going to lie about it. She shook her head and made it clear she didn't feel comfortable with my occupation.

It was okay with me. I was used to being judged for being an intuitive advisor; this wasn't anything new. I found it humorous. I ended up moving into a fantastic little cottage that was bright and shiny with lots of faeries and flowers surrounding it. It stood off by itself in a grove of trees and was within walking distance of town.

A couple of weeks later, after I had already moved into my new digs, I got a phone call from the lady who had refused to rent me the other cottage. She told me she thought it over and had changed her mind. She went on to explain that when she was young, she was involved in similar thinking and tried to make it in a profession quite similar to mine. She was discouraged by the negative and disparaging judgments of other people. She admitted she let her own fear and unresolved issues interfere with her decision about renting her cottage to me.

Business was good and I was updating some promotional and advertising media. I needed a new professional picture. There was a sweet little gal I knew who had a friend who was a professional photographer.

This little gal was very industrious and I thought it would be good to send some business their way. We happily set up a time to meet.

The morning of the appointment, while I was enjoying my coffee, I got this hit to give her a call. It felt to me the photo shoot was not going to take place. When she answered, I could tell she was very uncomfortable with what she was about to tell me. She said she was sorry, but she and her friend couldn't help me because of their belief system. They were both Christians, and didn't feel comfortable putting their names on photos that would be used to promote ideas and activities they viewed as being in conflict with their faith. I totally understood and was okay with it. I knew another photographer who would do my promo shots and for less money than I intended to pay them. I was just trying to be being nice in giving them the business.

I was a bit sad, but didn't take it personally. I had experience with dealing with people's judgments of my lifestyle and work. I think my sadness had more to do with this little gal and what seemed like her own confusion and inability to accept herself. More than once I had witnessed situations in which she judged and beat herself up for one thing or another. She seemed to be having a hard time. I commend her for sticking up for her beliefs and making the decision to be conscious of her choices.

These two incidents occurring so close together encouraged me to believe in myself and to continue to love and honor myself. I knew I could write what was in my heart in hopes my sharing would help others to recognize the perfection within. In God's eyes we are perfect, no matter what we have put ourselves through by choice, or by acting as a victim. I received more confirmation that very night.

I thought back to my angel reading that morning. The "Come Out of the Closet" card had come up again. I used a deck of 300 cards compiled of multiple decks and miscellaneous cards I had collected through the years. This particular card had come up every day for the past week, sometimes in readings I did for myself, but also in readings I did for others. I began to realize this card was important, not only for my clients, but for me as well. My guides wanted me to get the message. It was time to listen. It was more than chance this card was appearing so many times. Nevertheless, I was boggled. Why would "Come Out of the Closet" keep coming up? It didn't make any sense. It was getting quite funny. This card came up more than it had ever come up in the several years of using the cards. What in the world did I need to come out of the closet for? I kept asking and wondering but nothing came to mind.

Now mind you, at the same time I am struggling with what direction to take my writing. Do I go fiction and insert bits of real live magic into it? Do I talk about my relationships, which collectively constitutes an extensive educational manual all by itself? Do I write about my life and the trials and tribulations even though I might very well open the floodgates to more criticism and judgment? I kept going around and around and screech! All of a sudden I stopped and it dawned on me. It was as if a bolt of lightning struck me. You know that "ah ha" moment when something finally clicks. I was to come out of the closet with my worst fears. I was to share some of my own personal judgments, the ones more critical than I ever received from others. I was to share what I have wanted to share, but didn't know how, or was unwilling to because of my own judgment of myself.

If others were going to judge me harshly for being a light in this world, then so be it. I felt the pain of being judged, ostracized and belittled for choosing my life as an intuitive advisor. In reality I was being judged for walking my talk and speaking my truth. My judges were people full of fear themselves. I did not have the power to change their thinking, but I have the power to change my own. These revelations helped me get clear on why and how I was going to tell my story. I would just tell it like it is, and most importantly, I would do it feeling good about myself. Wasn't that what it's all about anyway? Loving Thyself no matter what? God loves us no matter what. It was time for me to lay aside my self-judgment and Come Out of the Closet!

Imagination is where it all begins. When we want to change something in our lives, we begin by taking the time to dream and imagine what is possible. Otherwise, we may not be clear about where we want to go. For years I have imagined myself in Ireland. I wasn't sure why, but I knew Ireland would be a very important part of my journey.

My relationship with the faeries was one thing which motivated me to visit Ireland. This country has a long and colorful tradition of faerie lore. Ireland is where faerie history begins and continues to this day with people honoring the faeries with regular offerings and gifts. Irish music has always been a joy for me. It transports me to another period – a time of joy and dancing and freedom. Before moving into the town of Friday Harbor, my roommate and I shared our dreams of visiting Ireland one day. I wanted to visit the faeries; he wanted to sweep the author of a seaweed cookbook off her feet and live happily ever after.

After being up in the San Juan Islands for a year, I felt antsy and questioned whether or not I wanted to stay another winter season on an island so far from civilization. It is an hour ferry ride between the island and the mainland. Even though I loved the reclusiveness of the island and the slower pace of life, I wasn't clear about wanting to stay longer. I had come to the island to write and finish my book. Even though I recorded many thoughts and ideas, I still had not connected the dots and woven the ideas together into a story. Island life and being alone had presented some incredible opportunities for self-growth and spiritual insights.

Although, as before I kept quite busy, living on the island was different. The quiet and solitude were conducive to reflection and inner awakening. I quit beating myself up for working so much. In the midst of solitude, magic was more tangible. I felt closer to God. But at the same time, I was receiving signs it might be time for a change. Job offers off island were appearing.

These made me seriously rethink whether or not I wanted to stay another year. Was spirit asking me to move on, and if so, where was I supposed to move to? The previous winter was a barren and solitary one. When the tourists leave, the spa is less busy. I worked at home a lot through the winter, as an intuitive advisor on the hotline. I wondered if this was what was in store for me during the coming winter.

I could say my ego was telling me to move because of finances. I could make more off island in the winter months than if I stayed. So I went with that as an excuse. When the opportunity arose to move in with one of my girlfriends who lived just south of Seattle I took it. Sharing expenses would help both of us reach financial goals, mine being to pay off my debt. I thought it would be a winning situation for both of us. I would virtually cut my expenses to less than half of what I was spending. It sounded like a good idea.

I started packing and preparing. Over the years the saying "it is far easier to steer a car that is moving than one that is stationary" has certainly been true for me. If you feel you should move on or take action, even when you are unsure of the goal, trust and the path and destination will become clear after you hit the road. It is much like "Jump and the net will appear".

While living on the island I met a new hiking friend. He was visiting one of his children who had recently moved to the island. He had been divorced for 20 years and his ex-wife had passed away quite suddenly almost a year before. I believe our paths were destined to cross. The first time I met him on the island to go for a hike, was the anniversary of the day the FBI knocked on my door so many years before.

We stood in my kitchen as I fixed lunch before our hike. There were several family photos posted on the refrigerator, including a picture of Sam, Shawn and me, taken on one of our visits to see him in prison. This man had worked in law enforcement during the time of the case; and he recognized Sam in the photo. A jolt of shock shot through my body when he said his name. I asked him if he knew the case and he said "yes, it was a very widely known case." Suddenly I remembered the date and was reminded it was the same day as the FBI visit years before. Another shock went through my body.

I had been struggling at that point with my writing and whether or not I would write about the story. I had always avoided finding out about the case and wished to have nothing to do with it. Perhaps the time had come to re-exam that entire episode of my life. It could facilitate further healing and validate the role of my intuition at that time.

After he left I called my friend Karen who was very familiar with my struggle with content for my book. I pointed out the amazing synchronicity of my new friend, who was familiar with the case and just happened to come to my house on the anniversary of a date I will never forget. She too felt a shock move through her body as I shared this new turn of events. We could both feel an eerie energy on both sides of the phone. I was very distraught. This entire situation that I tried so hard to forget was re-surfacing and I knew I was being asked to share it in my book. Karen calmed me by assuring me I didn't have to write about Sam if I didn't want to. I felt temporarily relieved knowing my intuition was pushing me to pursue it. But in the moment I could put it on the back burner and quit stewing over it. However, the relief was minimal and temporary as this pot was anything but quiet; it was making enough noise I was unable to keep it out of my consciousness.

One day before I moved off the island I met with my new friend to go hiking. I was aware of messages coming through from his deceased ex-wife. She wanted to communicate, but not with him, with me. She thought it would be a good idea for me to get involved with her ex-husband. She had loved him dearly and had held onto hope for reconciliation but it was not to be.

He and I hiked to Jakle's Lagoon, one of my favorite island hikes. I could feel her presence. It seemed strange I kept hearing her name and thinking about her, but I attributed it to the fact he had recently shared some things about his life with her and we discussed some of the unresolved concerns he had about their relationship. I sat down on the ridge with an encompassing view that included a glimpse of Mt. Rainier about 126 miles in the distance. I began to pray and acknowledge my spirit guides, giving thanks to all that is. I felt very blessed to be in such a wonderful part of the world. I truly loved going up to the ridge and sitting for hours in the warm sunshine where I could hear the faint singing of the whales if I listened deeply.

In this quiet place she came through to me expressing concern about his loneliness and depression. She didn't want him to be alone and she believed I could help him spiritually. He and I could not have been any more different. He had a background in law enforcement and years spent in the military. He played the stock market every day and loved watching the news. He recorded every crime show televised so he could watch them at his leisure. I rarely watched television, maybe once in a blue moon. And if I did watch something, it was likely to be a love story on the Hallmark Channel. I live for the silence of the woods, not the chatter of television. I didn't even own one, and hadn't had one for years. I did not concern myself with money or planning for my future, let alone understand how the stock market worked. Our spiritual beliefs were far apart as well. The only things we seemed to have in common were the love of playing the game Ace Duce and hiking.

The information coming through seemed to be coming from spirit and I started thinking I should take it into consideration. I wasn't getting any younger and I was tired of living my life alone. I was far from lonely but really desired a companion. I decided maybe a relationship with him could work. I was part of a large spiritual community; maybe I didn't need a spiritual connection with a partner. He made me an offer that boiled down to something like me being a kept woman. I have to admit, it was tempting. I wouldn't have to work so hard. I could spend as much time as I wanted writing.

I would have time to be with me. I would get to visit Ireland because of one of his children was living there. I asked for guidance and questioned the authenticity of the messages I was picking up from his deceased wife. Was she correct in her assessment of him and of our compatibility? Later that evening I talked with my friend Karen, who is also a professional psychic. She mentioned her mom by name. I about fell off the chair because her mom has the same, very uncommon, name as my friend's deceased ex-wife! I had my validation. My friend's wife was indeed communicating with me. But still, the phrase "fitting a square peg into a round hole" repeated in my mind each time I thought about taking our relationship to the next level.

Deceased loved ones mean well. They only want us to be cared for in a manner they think best. I have learned through the years it is very important to remember when communicating with deceased spirits, you must establish boundaries and ask God, his helpers the ascended masters, and angels, for guidance to find the highest good for all. Sometimes we feel compelled to act on a message simply because it comes from the spirit world. In many ways, we should treat these messages the same as advice from a friend and not automatically give it special importance. It is the messages that come from God that really matter. It is our intuition we must listen to.

I made arrangements to move off the island and move in with my girlfriend as planned. It didn't take long for me to realize the situation was not working. I was going through a bit of shell shock coming from a quiet island into a neighborhood in south Seattle, filled with the noise of cars, airplanes and people almost twenty-four hours a day. But also, I found our lifestyles were radically different and the overstimulation sent me into anxiety attacks. She thrived on noise. First thing in the morning the radio blared. In every room there was noise or she was talking. We had been friends for many years and she was doing her best to accommodate my needs, but it wasn't working.

I needed quiet. Being in the city was proving to be quite overwhelming. So I decided to take my Ace Duce friend up on his offer of moving in with him, but only as roommates. He was happy with this arrangement. In fact he was exploring other dating options. He was just as quick to realize a round hole wasn't suitable for a square peg. Neither of us wanted to force a romantic relationship, and meanwhile, we could help each other out. He had a huge home and gave me my own bedroom, office and bathroom. I could write as often and as long as I wanted, and could participate in hot yoga sessions at a center right down the street. We had an agreement. I could live rent-free in exchange for helping him freshen up the place with paint and some remodeling, play Ace Duce with him, and go on an occasional hike.

This sounded like a dream come true, especially after the shell shock of moving off the island. I could focus on me and my goals without interruption and save some money at the same time. There was also a beautiful view of Mt. Rainier in all her glory from the living room. He lived on a very quiet street out in the country. But this move was only temporary. I kept my eyes open for a condo. I wasn't sure about where I wanted to live next, but I had the freedom to take as long as I needed to find it. We laughed over our brief thoughts of "making it work" and fitting a round peg in a square hole for comfort's sake.

Even when things seem to sound good on the surface, it is so important to listen to what is being felt inside. Because we realized this and followed our intuition and didn't proceed with what his deceased wife had suggested, he is happily married to a wonderful gal who suits him perfectly. (I am sure his 'deceased wife' is very happy.)

Now that I lived off island it was a lot easier to do things like connecting with like-minded friends. I was also geographically closer to my family which was very nice. I kept my eyes open for the perfect place in the perfect area for my next home. I knew I wanted to live by the water and it had to have salt in it, so I was looking along the Sound from Olympia towards Seattle. I wondered where I would land.

I knew moving out on my own would mean going back to work at a spa and money might be a little tighter. I also wouldn't have as much time to write, but it had to be done. I scrolled through Craigslist a few times looking for something I could afford and asked myself "where do I want to live?" It turned out my body and soul was happiest when I envisioned living in the same area near the water where Shawn and I had lived in our little apartment years ago.

I noticed a condo by the water but it was more than I wanted to pay. It sounded wonderful, but I moved on to other ads, but didn't see anything else that really excited me. I wanted to be within walking distance of the water or better yet, have a view as I enjoyed my morning coffee. I knew my budget would limit my choices and I probably would have to forego the water view.

A couple weeks passed and I noticed the condo by the water was still available. I decided to make an appointment to take a look at it, although, I wasn't planning on getting it. I mostly just wanted to get some energy going. I was letting the universe know I was open and ready for things to shift in my life. I fell in love with it. It was tiny but had recently been remodeled and updated and even came with a mold free certificate. The big picture window in the living room looked out over the Puget Sound. I could definitely see myself here. I told the manager, I was just looking and the condo was out of my price range. He smiled at me and his eyes sparkled. He cupped his hands together and held them out to me and said, "Lacey, here is the net, jump!" I was startled by what he said. That morning I had written "if a net appears I am ready to jump."

The whole meeting with the manager felt surreal. I suspected he was really an angel. He had a gentle way about him that was caring and magical. I liked him instantly. I admitted to him that as much as I wanted to jump, I couldn't see a way to afford the rent. I explained I hadn't been working in the three months since I left the island. A background check would reveal my income during the last few months was not enough to cover the rent. He repeated, "Lacey the net is here. I'm not going to let you fall. Why don't you fill out the application and we will see what happens."

I took a deep breath and thought "what do I have to lose?" Even if the application was approved, I could still turn it down. I filled out the application and we said our goodbyes. We hugged each other, which was very interesting since we had just met. It seemed a little funny in retrospect. It was as if I had known this guy before. As I drove away, I decided to check out the job opportunities in the area. There were plenty of massage positions available, but I wasn't too excited. I wanted to get out of the field and move toward my bigger goal.

A couple of days later, I had my choice of several different massage jobs. I chose to take a position as a massage therapist at a chiropractor's office that was close to the condo. Even though I had not heard from the manager, I thought energetically it would let the universe know I was serious about living in the area. Hours after accepting the position, the manager of the condo emailed me with congratulations and the news I could move in after putting up the first and last months' rent along with a security deposit. "Well there you go!" I thought. It was fun dreaming while it lasted. I didn't have that kind of money just lying around. I smiled and thought, "Something else will show up; the Universe knows I am serious. I am willing to work some place that really isn't in alignment with what I want to do, and I am making the effort."

The thought kept coming into my mind that someone would be happy to give me a loan for the sum I needed to get into the condo. I felt the universe was also assuring me, if I did get the money to move in, I would somehow be able to make the rent, pay off the loan and the rest of my bills. I would be able to stay on track with the goal of being debt free within a year. This was something I had been working on for the past few years. I didn't want to be tied to my bills. I also decided, especially since I was not involved in a serious relationship, it would be fun to pay everything off, buy a van, and move down to the warmer climate of New Mexico where I could work in a healing center.

That was, if I didn't meet the man of my dreams before then. I had pretty much given up on the idea since I had spent years diligently working on this goal without a satisfactory and happy result. I could always settle, but I didn't really see that as a viable option. Living my life happily ever after with just me sounded pretty good at the moment.

I got a personal loan for the money I needed and started enjoying my life in my wonderful condo. I loved waking up and watching the big cargo ships floating by. The sound of airplanes in the distance melted into the background and I got used to it. I could hear my neighbors above and beside me but wasn't bothered. I had my own space and was surrounded by my own things. I sorted through boxes of stuff that had been packed away for a couple years. I was getting rid of things I no longer needed or wanted. I was simplifying my life.

I accepted a second job so drove one direction a couple times a week and drove the other direction the other days. I worked every day but I didn't mind. I was living in my own space and loving it. I found I made the rent super early in the month and sent the rest of my payments a couple weeks ahead of schedule. I wanted the manager to know I was trusting my own process and making it, thanks to him putting the net out.

For the past several years I had hosted a number of radio shows, my latest one focused on talking to my audience about healing, inspiration, and self empowerment. I invited guests to join me who also shared how to live a healthier life. I loved doing radio, but with the pressure of two new jobs, I reluctantly let the "Groovy Green Goddess" radio program go. I continued my work with the psychic hot-line providing intuitive readings. I knew cutting back on the radio was only temporary for it was very dear to my heart and was a part of my ultimate goal to help and support others. For now, I wanted as much time as possible to devote to my writing and doing the weekly radio show was taking more time than I wanted to give.

What happened next still blows my mind when I think about it. I was happily going through my days working and writing, and did I mention working? I was also finding time to spend with my family and friends and entertaining them in my humble little abode. I had signed a year's lease and was comfortably settled in, excited about knowing I had landed for a year. Life was good, my sons were grown and stable and I had a working plan to pay off my debts. By the time the year was over, I'd know what my next plan of action would be.

Before moving off the island several months earlier, I decided to experiment with dating in a new context. I started dating in groups and attended activities and events especially for singles in my area. My goal was to hopefully meet someone in a more natural environment instead of in a bar or through work. These social gatherings gave me the chance to observe how the men interacted with the women. The events were fun and I met a lot of great people.

At the same time, I had my profile up on an internet dating site I had been using since early 2005. My profile described me as someone who talks to faeries and angels every day and to borrow a phrase, "I see dead people." Needless to say I often attracted men who wanted me to communicate with their dead wives, or who wanted to know about their future and if I was in it. Most were not contenders, totally out of the ball park when it came to what I was looking for in a partner. I suppose I continued to keep my profile posted so I could feel good when someone indicated interest in me. More often than not, the attraction was not mutual, but their attention did help lift my self esteem.

One Friday night I was bored and went online to see who might have looked at my profile. There was someone, but their profile lacked a photo. Normally I would not even consider an individual who didn't post a photo. But they caught my attention with the catch line at the top of the profile indicating they were living in Ireland. My curiosity was piqued. I opened his profile and began reading. His writing style was intellectually stimulating and creative. He seemed open to possibilities and to what the universe had to offer. I sent a note and on a whim, asked him if he'd seen many faeries in Ireland.

A couple days went by and I got a reply. His letter was more than I could have imagined or hoped for. It was delightful to read and yes, he had met a faerie or two in his life, and we were not talking about gay men. He explained he was new to the site and had delayed his response, so he would have time to get his photo posted. When I saw his pictures, I was sure I knew him. He looked very familiar and I wondered if we had met before. The feeling was very intense. We started writing back and forth and all the while I kept telling myself nothing would come of this. After all we were on different continents. He was clear over in Ireland and I was in Washington State. I kept reminding myself to not get attached. This correspondence was just for fun. And indeed it was fun to communicate with someone far away who also believed in faeries.

It didn't take long for both of us to realize there was something special going on here. It was very different from the email interactions I'd had with others on the site. We had so much in common. We aspired towards similar dreams. He also wanted to travel around in a van throughout the U.S. He had traveled in the states on two previous occasions.

It was also very hard to deny the magic happening around us. He was eight hours ahead of me on the clock. Sometimes I would be lying in bed thinking of something I wanted to say to him or a question I wanted to ask. I'd make a note to remind myself to ask him the next morning. I'd wake up to an email with the answer to the question I had not yet posed! He was in my head and I was in his. One time I was thinking about my attitudes toward drugs and medications. I didn't want to be involved in a relationship with someone who relied heavily on prescription pills or was addicted to the same, especially if they were taking them for emotional illnesses. I wanted to be with someone who believed in self-healing and who didn't use prescription drugs as a crutch. I woke up to an endearing email echoing my sentiments, but in a very creative and humorous way.

He said he had heard it was compulsory in America to take some form of prescription medication; and he asked me if I was taking Prozac since I heard voices and saw visions. He also mentioned he cycled into town every day to keep healthy and the only thing he took was vitamins. I fell in love with him right then and there. (I guess my history demonstrates I fall in love very easily!)

We started dating via Skype and left each other daily video greetings and notes about our days. We agreed it would be nice to really date each other sometime in the future. To my surprise, thirteen days after I asked him if he had ever met any faeries, he purchased a plane ticket to Seattle. He planned to arrive in three weeks.

The Irish man arrived and immediately we got along like a house on fire. As soon as I saw him at the airport I knew he was it. We got along better than I had ever gotten along with anyone in my life. It was as if we had been long lost friends coming together to finish our journey. I was still working like a mad woman during his visit but we made time to get outdoors and just be together. We ate out and took long walks along the Puget Sound exchanging life stories and amazing ourselves with all the experiences and interests we had in common. He too was interested in personal growth, had worked in management positions, and even worked for a time managing a women's refuge shelter. He was familiar with addictions and the huge commitment required by an individual to overcome them.

He was open to whatever the Universe had in store for him, just like me. He was a dreamer and understood my dreamer ways. We talked for hours about metaphysics and shared ideas from the books we had read. He loved writing and reading, two of my passions. When I talked about my guides and experiences with Andy, my alien friend, he listened intently and I could feel his genuine understanding and non-judgment.

My Irish man and I talked about traveling together, maybe even buying a van and touring the states. We also discussed the possibility of my going over to Ireland to visit him. But I also explained my plan to stay put and pay off my bills. I had signed the one-year lease on the condo just three months earlier. The relationship seemed to be moving very quickly and my commitment to my plan and to my condo seemed to act as a safety net for both of us until we got to know each other better.

We were a little concerned about the idea of a long distance relationship. We had both been involved in these kinds of relationships before and found it didn't work. However, we were willing to see what would happen. We made a conscious choice to live in the moment and release the need to know today, what would unfold tomorrow.

A couple of days prior to my Irish man's arrival, while giving the apartment a good cleaning, I found mold on my couch. I put it out of my mind, being so busy getting ready for his visit, keeping up my work schedule and spending time with my sister who had come up for the weekend. There wasn't room in my mind to give the mold much thought. During his stay I went to get some clothes out of the back of my closet. With a new boyfriend, I had a good excuse to wear some of my glitzy clothes. To my dismay, I found some of the clothes were damp and had mold on them. The back wall of the closet was covered in mold.

The manager came to take a look at the mold. He apologized for the inconvenience and explained there had been a leak on the roof with water draining between the condo wall and the outside wall. In order to fix the leak and get rid of the mold, I needed to leave the apartment for two or three weeks. He offered to break the lease and refund my last month's rent and security deposit if that was my choice, no questions asked.

I stood listening in disbelief. Just a few days before my Irish friend and I had been joking about my being released from the contract so we could be together. I really didn't think it would be this easy. This was the Universe's way of saying "this is the chance of a lifetime, take it!" And I did.

The Irish man flew back to Ireland, but not before buying a van we could travel in during the summer. Within a couple of weeks I was out of my apartment. I sold things I had contemplated selling for a couple of years but hadn't yet. I gave whatever else I didn't need away to friends. For years I had been working on simplifying my life and now I had the perfect excuse to do so. I put some of my cherished belongings in storage, such as my crystal ball and leprechaun cane. I placed Bamboo Bob, my dear bamboo plant, in the care of my sister. With no more rent to pay I finished paying off my debts. I couch surfed for the next month getting my affairs in order. A month later I was in Ireland.

AFTER THOUGHTS

We learn to have faith in the connection we have with source therefore we strengthen our belief. We can live according to our hearts' desires. I felt the calling to assist others in finding the faith and confidence for themselves. When I landed my corporate job and was able to live near the water, my confidence soared. Of course I had days when I plummeted back into the scared little girl not knowing what I was doing, how I was going to make it financially, and where I was going.

What I have finally learned is, I don't have to know where I am going as long as I have a wide vision of my goal. My mantra is "This or Something Better!" I also remember God has a plan for all of us, and his plan is always bigger and grander than the plan we see for ourselves. Success is a matter of believing. So many times through the years I have witnessed myself as well as others, losing faith and not being able to see or believe in a higher plan. This keeps us stuck in the same old patterns. Another thing I have learned is to enjoy the process and remember the journey is often more important than achieving the goal.

As I learned to love myself and to not judge myself or others, I found things started getting better in my life. I felt more confident that sharing my life lessons was valuable for others.

A dear friend of mine made a suggestion one day about those thoughts that come from the ego. She said, "Lacey, the next time your ego starts talking to you like that, get out a sock, put eyes on it and a mouth, and put it on your hand and anytime your ego wants to say things you know are not true, talk to the sock. It will keep the moment light and you will quickly remember how silly our ego will act sometimes."

I believe God is here for us all the time and it is up to us to recognize that. It's not like he stands in front of us and waves his arms and says, "Hey you need to get a grip!" Although looking back at different events that have taken place in my life, God was definitely waving and trying to get my attention. It was up to me to recognize the waving and do something about it.

It is important we do not let what others think about us override our opinions of ourselves. This can be difficult. As humans we tend to take on the thinking and attitudes of people surrounding us. It's wise to choose our environments carefully and if necessary, limit or avoid contact with people and situations we know will bring our energy down. Of course there are many people we cannot or maybe do not want to avoid, like family members, bosses, and etc. If their influence tends to be negative, we may have to work just a little bit harder to deflect their negativity and judgments. It's certainly easier to maintain a positive attitude and strong self-confidence when I'm not using my energy to defend myself; therefore when necessary I choose to limit contact with people who do not support me. At times, I have found it hard enough to be gentle with myself; I don't need the added stress of being around judgmental people and circumstances.

It helps to remember the Golden Rule, "Treat others like we want to be treated." Everyone is equal in the eyes of God even if our religions, belief systems and lifestyles are vastly different. As we respect ourselves, we will respect others. And nicely enough, it works the other way around too! We are all on our individual paths.

Keeping an open mind and respecting other people's right to choose their own way goes a long way toward insuring a happy and contented life. Love your neighbor and practice non-judgment.

Going to church or belonging to a program or an interest group that supports you in a positive way can be an important way to learn and to create a sense of belonging to something bigger than yourself. So is going out into the great outdoors and being with God. Do what resonates with your soul and feeds the divinity within. Without an understanding of a higher power that goes beyond us, we cannot know ourselves, for we are made in God's image. Understanding God through our own means is the only way we can discover the very core of our inner self.

Some of the ways we can explore our higher power is to pray; and it doesn't have to be in a formal prayer. Just saying "Hey, you up there, over there, or where ever, I would like to know you better. I would like to know if you are even there. I appreciate any counsel you can give." It is as simple as that. God doesn't need a lot of fanfare.

It is our human mind that makes it seem like a big and pompous event. Of course we like rituals, celebrations and coming together to bring in a power bigger than ourselves for healing, and that is all good. It is also acceptable to God that we do it silently, alone and simple. It is what resonates with you that is important. Besides, we are never alone even when we think we are.

Along with prayer, we can quiet our minds and connect through meditation. Take time to listen. Silencing our minds and letting go of all the busyness and stress we encounter in our daily lives is good for our spiritual well being. Sitting in silence and meditation will often bring the answers we have been seeking. It takes patience and diligence; so don't give up. The changes that occur sometimes happen on a very subtle level and sometimes can happen quite suddenly and traumatically. But that too is part of the process. Change is constant. If we are willing to do what is called upon by God, we have to be ready to roll with the changes that come our way and seek to understand the meaning.

Nothing is as it seems. On our way to dreams being fulfilled we may have to clean house. We have to make sure we stay in our own back yard when wanting something to occur in our lives. When we wish for something that involves another person, we have to "Let go and let God". There is always a calm that happens after a storm. It isn't easy to let go of people, places and things that no longer serve our highest interest or calling, but we must do so in order to be free to draw closer to an understanding of our own journey and higher self which is really the God or Goddess within.

I believe we are all called to develop and use our gifts of intuition. It's important for everyone to learn to use whatever gifts God has given them for the greater good. We can all discover and improve our intuition. It takes courage, but there are teachers to help.

What I have learned about getting to know thyself is that perseverance is the key. We have to "keep on, keepin on", no matter what. If one day we feel down, the next day or the next hour we have to pull ourselves back up. Do the action often enough and the feelings will follow or put another way, "fake it until we make it!" Positive affirmations and dwelling on the good and beautiful helps. We have to remember some days may be a bit more challenging than others and sharing problems you have with someone will help.

The more I live life and work through my personal experiences, the more I am convinced it takes some sort of belief in a higher power to fill what may feel like a void within us. It doesn't necessarily matter what that looks like, but it's important to come from a place of love and non-judgment. The vision I get when I think of religion is a bicycle wheel with all the metal spokes connecting to the center hub. They are all going to the same place. Each spoke represents a different belief system or way a person can practice religion. Some spokes may be bent out of shape or have a little rust on them but they are all hoping to reach the center. I also believe in order to understand fully the evolution of man, it is a good idea to know a little, or a lot in some cases, about each spoke thus giving a deeper understanding.

Being open minded is also very important. The bottom line is Love is what makes the world go round and just because I don't call myself a Christian, a Pagan or Jew doesn't mean I reject what they believe. It is very important we all get along and only think good thoughts about our neighbors. We really don't know what a person has gone through until we have walked a mile in their shoes. It is very important not to judge.

I believed for a long time I would share my story some day. I would get the push to move forward and then something would stop me. I was full of fear. Often I remained unaware of my fear by covering it up with busyness and staying active 24/7. I was productive from an external point of view, but inside, that was really a different story. "Yikes what if so and so knew 'that part' of my life? They would think it was pure stupidity." The path I walked has been invaluable to me in my work. My experiences have helped me understand and appreciate what others are going through and the choices and paths they take. My counseling and other services are enriched by my personal journey and experiences.

It is indeed the sum of all our experiences that create the whole person we are. It took time for me to recognize my patterns and that I was making the same ill-advised choices over and over again. But the universe never ceased to reach out to me through divine circumstances and others' timely intervention showing me there was a better way and I was worthy of a better life. But it was still up to me to do all the hard work even at this point of writing the book. I was afraid I would be judged by what my experiences were and how I approached life and what I had gone through. I was scared people would point their finger towards me and I would have to become a hermit and avoid public life. I started realizing even the people closest to me may not like what I had to say and that my speaking my truth might sow discord. But I knew I had been called to write about these experiences. Not for me alone but to motivate and to help others going through the same or similar experience to get help and to open themselves up to trust their own intuition and to help others find their way out of situations and that they are worthy. I also procrastinated, waiting for my life to become perfect or at times waiting to have a perfect place with a perfect view (which I manifested many times during this process). If only such and such happened, then I would be able to sit down and spread myself out and begin to write. I also delayed writing, by thinking I needed to be in a place by myself. But eventually I just had to trust it was the perfect time and trust the guidance of my higher power, God, the Angels, and the Ascended Masters, and to continue to pray and have faith, and put all these experiences down in writing for all those called to read it.

It is indeed an amazing and magical Universe we are all part of and if nothing else in writing this book it has once again reminded me everything and everyone – all life is connected. We are all indeed on every level connected.

ABOUT THE AUTHOR

Lacey has been a student of Metaphysics for over 35 years and in the healing arts professionally for over 25. She is an internationally known Intuitive Advisor inspiring and motivating her clients through 12listen.com, a premiere psychic hotline, and through in person sessions conducted during her travels. She hosts a radio program "Groovy Green Goddess" and holds classes and support groups worldwide.

She is passionate when it comes to helping others become the best they can be. Her passion is to work with women who have been in abusive relationships or who have struggled with addictions, because she understands what it takes to motivate oneself to break the cycle. Lacey also works as a health coach teaching people how to take better care of themselves through sound principles of eating and exercise, and more fully integrating body, mind, heart and spirit.

Lacey is working on her latest book, "7 Steps to Finding Your Authentic Self" to be published in 2015. This book begins where this one left off as well as going through 7 steps to Empowerment.
Lacey also has other books in the works, "When My Boyfriend Let Me Back Into the Van" and "Groovy 'Green' Goddess: Health Matters!" Both coming in 2016.

Lacey's gypsy spirit prompts her to live in the beautiful Northwest as well as traveling abroad. You can find her by going to her website: LaceyDawnJackson.com

Check out her YouTube channel Lacey Dawn Jackson, Facebook page LaceyDawnJacksonPsychic & Groovy Green Goddess.

Lacey is available for speaking engagements as well as Intuitive coaching and Inspiration.

Email Lacey at lacey@laceydawnjackson.com

www.ingramcontent.com/pod-product-compliance
Lightning Source LLC
Chambersburg PA
CBHW061425040426
42450CB00007B/912